CROCHET

Fashion Doll Collection, Book 2™

General Information

Many of the products used in this pattern book can be purchased from local craft, fabric and variety stores, or from the Annie's Attic Needlecraft Catalog *(see Customer Service information on page 63).*

BARBIE® and associated trademarks are owned by and used with permission from Mattel, Inc. ©2005 Mattel, Inc.

Cozy Evenings

Designs by Joyce Bishop

CHAISE LOUNGE

SKILL LEVEL

INTERMEDIATE

FINISHED SIZE

9 inches long x 6 inches tall

MATERIALS

- ❏ Medium (worsted) weight yarn: 1½ oz/75 yds/43g variegated
- ❏ Size G/6/4mm crochet hook or size needed to obtain gauge
- ❏ Tapestry needle
- ❏ Large sheet stiff clear 7-count plastic canvas

GAUGE

4 sc = 1 inch; 4 sc rows = 1 inch

INSTRUCTIONS

LOUNGE
Frame

1. From plastic canvas cut each of the following pieces:
Seat: 1 piece 55 x 20 holes
Sides: 2 pieces 55 x 15 holes
End: 1 piece 20 x 15 holes
Back: 1 piece 20 x 36 holes

2. With variegated, whipstitch *(see illustration below and diagram on page 3)* seat, end and side pieces tog. Holding back to assembled pieces, whipstitch matching holes to unworked short edges of side *(back will extend above seat area).*

3. Set aside to use later.

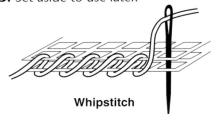

Whipstitch

Lounge Cover
Seat

Row 1: Ch 12, sc in 2nd ch from hook and in each ch across, turn. *(11 sc)*

Rows 2–31: Ch 1, sc in each st across, turn.

Row 32: Ch 1, sc in each st across, working in ends of rows, sc in each

BARBIE® and associated trademarks are owned by and used with permission from Mattel, Inc. ©2005 Mattel, Inc.

row across, working in starting ch on opposite side of row 1, sc in each ch across, working in ends of rows, sc in each row across, turn.

Rows 33–40: Ch 1, sc in each st across, turn. At end of last row, fasten off.

Back

Row 1: Starting at lower portion of back, ch 12, sc in 2nd ch from hook and in each ch across, turn. *(11 sc)*

Rows 2–8: Ch 1, sc in each st across, turn. At end of last row, fasten off.

Row 9: To extend width for arms, ch 15, sc in each st across row 8, ch 16, turn.

Row 10: Sc in 2nd ch from hook and in each ch and st across, turn. *(41 sc)*

Rows 11–25: Ch 1, sc in each st across, turn.

Row 26: Working in **back lps** *(see Stitch Guide)*, ch 1, sc in each st across, turn.

Rows 27–40: Ch 1, sc in each st across, turn. At end of last row, fasten off.

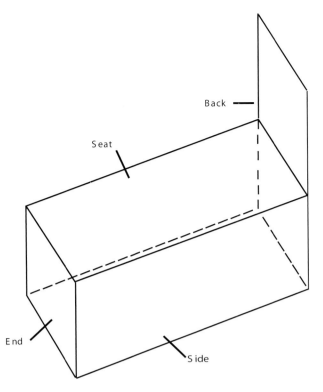

Assembly

1. Fold down row 26 with ridge formed by the back lps as the top, sew narrow ends tog at each side *(forms pocket)*.
2. Slip pocket formed by sewn piece over top of plastic canvas back piece. Place crocheted Seat over assembled plastic canvas Frame.
3. Sew rows 1–8 of Back to rows 34–40 of Seat. Sew row 32 of Seat to middle section of row 40 of Back.
4. Fold rem double thicknesses of Back over and tack edge to row 33 to secure.
5. Whipstitch row 40 of Seat and row 1 of Back to the unworked edge of the Frame.
6. Fold center of Back over plastic canvas and roll arms under, tack in place to secure *(see illustration)*.

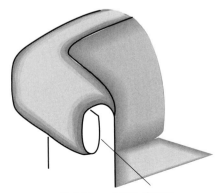

**Fold top edge down
& tack in place**

PILLOWS

SKILL LEVEL

EASY

FINISHED SIZES
Square pillow: 3½ inches across
Round pillow: 3¼ inches in diameter

MATERIALS
- ❑ Fine (sport) weight yarn:
  ¼ oz/23 yds/7g each
  burgundy and off-white
- ❑ Size E/4/3.5mm crochet hook
  or size needed to obtain gauge
- ❑ Size 2/2.20mm steel crochet hook
- ❑ Fiberfill

GAUGE
Size E hook: 5 sc rnds = 2 inches in diameter

INSTRUCTIONS
SQUARE PILLOW
Side
Make 2.

Rnd 1: With burgundy and size E hook, ch 2 loosely, 12 sc in 2nd ch from hook, join with sl st in beg sc. *(12 sc)*

Rnd 2: Ch 4 *(counts as first dc and ch 1)*, dc in same st, dc in each of next 2 sts, *(dc, ch 1, dc) in next st, dc in each of next 2 sts, rep from * around, join with sl st in 3rd ch of beg ch-4.

Rnd 3: Ch 3 *(counts as first dc)*, *(dc, ch 1, dc) in next ch sp**, dc in each of next 4 sts, rep from * around, ending last rep at **, dc in each of last 3 sts, join with sl st in 3rd ch of beg ch-3. Fasten off.

Rnd 4: Ch 3, dc in next st, *(2 dc, ch 1, 2 dc) in next ch sp**, dc in each of next 6 sts, rep from * around, ending last rep at **, dc in each of last 4 sts, join with sl st in 3rd ch of beg ch-3. Fasten off.

Holding sides WS tog and working through both thicknesses, with E hook, join off-white with sc in any st, sc in each st around with 3 sc in each ch-1 sp, stuffing with fiberfill before closing, join with sl st in beg sc. Fasten off.

Button
Make 2.

With off-white and size 2 steel hook, ch 3, 10 hdc in 3rd ch from hook, join with sl st in 3rd ch of beg ch-3. Fasten off.

Weave end through **back lps** *(see Stitch Guide)* of sts, tighten and sew 1 to each side of Pillow.

ROUND PILLOW
Side
Make 2.

Rnd 1: With off-white and size E hook, ch 2, 6 sc in 2nd ch from hook, join with sl st in beg sc. *(6 sc)*

Rnd 2: Ch 1, 2 sc in first st, 2 sc in each st around, join with sl st in beg sc. *(12 sc)*

Rnd 3: Ch 1, sc in first st, 2 sc in next st, [sc in next st, 2 sc in next st] around, join with sl st in beg sc. *(18 sc)*

Rnd 4: Ch 1, sc in each of first 2 sts, 2 sc in next st, [sc in each of next 2 sts, 2 sc in next st] around, join with sl st in beg sc. *(24 sc)*

Rnd 5: Ch 1, sc in each of next 3 sts, 2 sc in next st, [sc in each of next 3 sts, 2 sc in next st] around, join with sl st in beg sc. Fasten off. *(30 sc)*

Holding Sides WS tog and working through both thicknesses, join off-white with sc in any st, sc in each of next 3 sts, 2 sc in next st, [sc in each of next 4 sts, 2 sc in next st] around, stuffing with fiberfill before closing, join with sl st in beg sc. Fasten off.

Button
Make 2.
With burgundy and size 2 steel hook, ch 3, 10 hdc in 3rd ch from hook, join with sl st in 3rd ch of beg ch-3. Fasten off.

Weave end through back lps of sts, tighten and sew 1 to each side of Pillow.

Edging
With burgundy and size E hook, join with sc in any st, ch 3, sk next st, [sc in next st, ch 3, sk next st] around, join with sl st in beg sc. Fasten off.

RUG

SKILL LEVEL

EASY

FINISHED SIZE
3¾ inches long

MATERIALS
- ❑ Medium (worsted) weight yarn: small amount variegated
- ❑ Size G/6/4mm crochet hook or size needed to obtain gauge

GAUGE
4 sc = 1 inch; 4 sc rows = 1 inch

INSTRUCTIONS
RUG
Rnd 1: Ch 6, sc in 2nd ch from hook, sc in each of next 3 chs, 3 sc in last ch, working on opposite side of ch, sc in each of next 3 chs, 2 sc in last ch, join with sl st in beg sc. *(12 sc)*

Rnd 2: Ch 1, 2 sc in first st, sc in each of next 3 sts, 2 sc in next st, sc in next st, 2 sc in next st, sc in each of next 3 sts, 2 sc in next st, sc in last st, join with sl st in beg sc. *(16 sc)*

Rnd 3: Ch 1, 2 sc in first st, sc in each of next 5 sts, 2 sc in each of next 3 sts, sc in each of next 5 sts, 2 sc in each of last 2 sts, join with sl st in beg sc. *(22 sc)*

Rnd 4: Ch 1, 2 sc in each of first 2 sts, sc in each of next 6 sts, 2 sc in each of next 2 sts, sc in next st, 2 sc in each of next 2 sts, sc in each of next 6 sts, 2 sc in each of next 2 sts, sc in last st, join with sl st in beg sc. *(30 sc)*

Rnd 5: Ch 1, sc in first st, 2 sc in each of next 2 sts, sc in each of next 9 sts, 2 sc in each of next 2 sts, sc in each of next 2 sts, 2 sc in each of next 2 sts, sc in each of next 9 sts, 2 sc in each of next 2 sts, sc in last st, join with sl st in beg sc. Fasten off.

Fringe
Cut 76 strands from burgundy each 2¼ inches in length. Holding 2 strands tog, fold in half, pull fold through st, pull ends through fold. Tighten. Trim ends.

Fringe in every other st on last rnd.

AFGHAN

SKILL LEVEL

EASY

FINISHED SIZE
5¾ inches x 7¾ inches, excluding Fringe

MATERIALS
- ❑ Medium (worsted) weight yarn: small amount off-white
- ❑ Fine (sport) weight yarn: ½ oz/46 yds/14g burgundy
- ❑ Size F/5/3.75mm crochet hook or size needed to obtain gauge

GAUGE
1 shell = 1 inch; 2 shell rows = 1 inch

SPECIAL STITCH
Shell: (2 dc, ch 1, 2 dc) in next ch or ch sp.

INSTRUCTIONS
AFGHAN
Row 1: With burgundy, ch 39, **shell** *(see Special Stitch)* in 6th ch from hook *(first chs count as first dc)*, sk next 2 chs, dc in next ch, [sk next 2 chs, shell in next ch, sk next 2 chs, dc in next ch] across, turn. *(6 shells, 7 dc)*

Rows 2–6: Ch 3, [shell in next ch sp, dc in next dc] across, turn. At end of last row, fasten off.

Row 7: Working on opposite side of starting ch on row 1, join burgundy with sl st in first ch, ch 3 *(counts as first dc)*, [sk next 2 chs, shell in next ch *(should line up with shell on opposite side of ch)*, sk next 2 chs, dc in next ch] across, turn.

Rows 8–12: Ch 3, [shell in next ch sp, dc in next st] across, turn. At end of last row, fasten off.

Fringe
For each Fringe, cut 1 strand of off-white 3 inches in length, separate into 2 strands of 2-ply each, holding both tog, fold in half, pull fold through st, pull ends through fold. Tighten. Trim ends.

Evenly sp 22 Fringes across each end of Afghan. ❑❑

Her Poncho

Design by Ann Rovnak

SKILL LEVEL

EASY

FINISHED SIZE

Fits 11½-inch fashion doll

MATERIALS

- ❑ Crochet cotton size 10:
  50 yds MC
  30 yds CC
- ❑ Size 7/1.65mm steel crochet hook or size needed to obtain gauge

GAUGE

9 sc = 1 inch; 9 sc rows = 1 inch

PATTERN NOTE

Always begin in the first stitch.

INSTRUCTIONS

PONCHO

Rnd 1: With MC, ch 40, sl st in first ch to form ring, ch 1, [sc in each of next 19 chs, 3 sc in next ch] around, join with sl st in beg sc. *(44 sc)*

Rnd 2: Ch 1, [sc in next 20 sts, 3 sc in next st, sc in next st] around, join with sl st in beg sc. *(48 sc)*

Rnd 3: Ch 1, [sc in each of next 21 sts, 3 sc in next st, sc in each of next 2 sts] around, join with sl st in beg sc. *(52 sc)*

Rnd 4: Ch 1, [sc in each of next 23 sts, 3 sc in next st, sc in each of next 2 sts] around, join with sl st in beg sc. *(56 sc)*

Rnd 5: Ch 1, [sc in each of next 24 sts, 3 sc in next st, sc in each of next 3 sts] around, join with sl st in beg sc. *(60 sc)*

Rnd 6: Ch 1, [sc in each of next 25 sts, 3 sc in next st, sc in each of next 4 sts] around, join with sl st in beg sc. *(64 sc)*

Rnd 7: Ch 1, [sc in each of next 26 sts, 3 sc in next st, sc in each of next 5 sts] around, join with sl st in

BARBIE® and associated trademarks are owned by and used with permission from Mattel, Inc. ©2005 Mattel, Inc.

beg sc. *(68 sc)*

Rnd 8: Ch 1, [sc in each of next 27 sts, 3 sc in next st, sc in each of next 6 sts] around, join with sl st in beg sc. *(72 sc)*

Rnd 9: Ch 1, [sc in each of next 28 sts, 3 sc in next st, sc in each of next 7 sts] around, join with sl st in beg sc. *(76 sc)*

Rnd 10: Ch 1, [sc in each of next 30 sts, 3 sc in next st, sc in each of next 7 sts] around, join with sl st in beg sc. *(80 sc)*

Rnd 11: Ch 1, [sc in each of next 31 sts, 3 sc in next st, sc in each of next 8 sts] around, join with sl st in beg sc. *(84 sc)*

Rnd 12: Ch 1, [sc in each of next 32 sts, 3 sc in next st, sc in each of next 9 sts] around, join with sl st in beg sc. *(88 sc)*

Rnd 13: Ch 1, [sc in each of next 33 sts, 3 sc in next st, sc in each of next 10 sts] around, join with sl st in beg sc. Fasten off. *(92 sc)*

Rnd 14: Join CC with sl st in first st, ch 1, [sc in each of next 34 sts, 3 sc in next st, sc in each of next 11 sts] around, join with sl st in beg sc. *(96 sc)*

Rnd 15: Ch 1, [sc in each of next 35 sts, 3 sc in next st, sc in each of next 12 sts] around, join with sl st in beg sc. *(100 sc)*

Rnd 16: Ch 1, [sc in each of next 36 sts, 3 sc in next st, sc in each of next 13 sts] around, join with sl st in beg sc. Fasten off. *(104 sc)*

Rnd 17: Join MC with sl st in first st, ch 1, [sc in each of next 38 sts, 3 sc in next st, sc in each of next 13 sts] around, join with sl st in beg sc. *(108 sc)*

Rnd 18: Ch 1, [sc in each of next 39 sts, 3 sc in next st, sc in each of next 14 sts] around, join with sl st in beg sc. *(112 sc)*

Rnd 19: Ch 1, [sc in each of next 40 sts, 3 sc in next st, sc in each of next 15 sts] around, join with sl st in beg sc. Fasten off. *(116 sc)*

Fringe

For each Fringe, cut 2 strands CC 2½ inches long. With both strands held tog, fold in half, with RS facing, insert hook in st, pull fold through, pull ends through fold, tighten.

Place Fringe in each st around. ❑❑

Cotillion Hoop Gown

Gown design by Joyce Bishop
Purse design by Mary Jo Cook

SKILL LEVEL

INTERMEDIATE

FINISHED SIZE

Gown and Hat: Fit 11½-inch fashion doll

MATERIALS

- ❑ Fine (sport) weight pompadour yarn:
    - 3 oz/510 yds/85g each white and lavender
- ❑ Crochet cotton size 10:
    - 45 yds lavender
- ❑ Size E/4/3.5mm crochet hook or size needed to obtain gauge
- ❑ Size 6/1.80mm steel crochet hook
- ❑ Sewing needle
- ❑ Sewing thread
    - white
    - purple
- ❑ 9-inch-diameter metal ring
- ❑ 5 straight pins
- ❑ 4 small snaps
- ❑ 2½ yds print bias tape
- ❑ 1 yd ¾-inch-wide lace trim
- ❑ 2 yds ¼-inch-wide purple ribbon

GAUGE

Size E hook: 5 dc = 1 inch, 5 dc rows = 2 inches

PATTERN NOTES

Use size E hook and yarn for Gown and Hat.

Use size 6 steel hook and size 10 thread for Purse.

INSTRUCTIONS

Gown
Overskirt

Row 1: With lavender (see Pattern Notes), ch 18, sc in 2nd ch from hook and in each ch across, turn. (17 sc)

Row 2: Ch 3 (counts as first dc), dc in same st, [ch 2, sk next st, 3 dc in next st] 7 times, ch 2, sk next st, 2 dc in last st, turn.

BARBIE® and associated trademarks are owned by and used with permission from Mattel, Inc. ©2005 Mattel, Inc.

Row 3: Ch 3, dc in next st, [ch 3, dc in each of next 3 sts] 7 times, ch 3, dc in each of last 2 sts, turn.

Rnd 4: Working in rnds, ch 3, dc in next st, (dc, ch 3, dc) in next ch sp, *dc in each of next 3 sts, (dc, ch 3, dc) in next ch sp, rep from * 6 times, dc in next st, sk last st, join with sl st in 3rd ch of beg ch-3.

Rnds 5–8: Ch 3, dc in each st across to first ch sp, (dc, ch 3, dc) in first ch sp, *dc in each st across to next ch sp, (dc, ch 3, dc) in next ch sp, rep from * 6 times, dc in each st across, join with sl st in 3rd ch of beg ch-3.

Rnd 9: Ch 3, dc in each of next 6 sts, (dc, ch 4, dc) in next ch sp, *dc in each of next 13 sts, (dc, ch 4, dc) in next ch sp, rep from * 6 times, dc in each of last 6 sts, join with sl st in 3rd ch of beg ch-3.

Rnd 10: Ch 3, dc in each of next 5 sts, **dc dec** (see Stitch Guide) in next 2 sts, *ch 4, sc in next ch sp, ch 4, dc dec in next 2 sts**, dc in each of next 11 sts, dc dec in next 2 sts, rep from * around, ending last rep at **, dc in each of last 5 sts, join with sl st in 3rd ch of beg ch-3.

Rnds 11–15: Ch 3, dc in each st across to last 2 sts before first ch sp, dc dec in next 2 sts, ch 4, (sc, ch 4) in each ch sp across, *dc dec in next 2 sts, dc in each st across to last 2 sts before next ch sp, dc dec in next

2 sts, ch 4, (sc, ch 4) in each ch sp across, rep from * 6 times, dc dec in next 2 sts, dc in each st across, join with sl st in 3rd ch of beg ch-3. *(8 dc groups and 8 sets of 7 ch-4 sps at end of rnd 15)*

Rnd 16: Ch 2, dc in next st, *[ch 5, sc in next ch sp] 7 times, ch 5, dc dec in next 3 sts, rep from * 6 times, ch 5, dc dec in last st and *(sk beg ch-2)* 2nd st.

Rnd 17: Sl st in each of first 3 chs of first ch sp, sc in same ch sp, [ch 5, sc in next ch sp] around, join with ch 2, dc in top of beg sc forming last ch sp.

Rnd 18: [Ch 5, sl st in 3rd ch from hook, ch 2, sc in next ch sp] around ending with ch 2, join with sl st in top of joining dc. Fasten off.

Underskirt

Row 1: With white, ch 18, sc in 2nd ch from hook and in each ch across, turn. *(17 sc)*

Row 2: Ch 3, 2 dc in each of next 15 sts, dc in last st, turn. *(32 dc)*

Row 3: Ch 3, dc in same st, [dc in next st, 2 dc in each of next 2 sts] 10 times, dc in last st, turn. *(53 dc)*

Rnd 4: Working in rnds, ch 3, dc in each st around, join with sl st in 3rd ch of beg ch-3.

Rnd 5: Ch 3, [dc in each of next 3 sts, 2 dc in next st] around, join with sl st in 3rd ch of beg ch-3. *(66 dc)*

Rnd 6: Ch 3, [dc in each of next 4 sts, 2 dc in next st] around, join with sl st in 3rd ch of beg ch-3. *(79 dc)*

Rnd 7: Ch 3, [dc in each of next 5 sts, 2 dc in next st] around, join with sl st in 3rd ch of beg ch-3. *(92 dc)*

Rnd 8: Ch 3, dc in each of next 6 sts, 2 dc in next st, [dc in each of next 6 sts, 2 dc in next st] around, join with sl st in top of beg-3. *(105 dc)*

Rnd 9: Ch 3, dc in each of next 4 sts, [2 dc in next st, dc in each of next 4 sts] around, join with sl st in 3rd ch of beg ch-3. *(125 dc)*

Rnd 10: Ch 3, dc in each st around, join with sl st in 3rd ch of beg ch-3.

Rnd 11: Ch 3, dc in each of next 4 sts, [2 dc in next st, dc in each of next 5 sts] around, join with sl st in 3rd ch of beg ch-3. *(145 dc)*

Rnd 12: Ch 3, dc in each st around, join with sl st in 3rd ch of beg ch-3.

Rnd 13: Ch 3, dc in each of next 4 sts, [2 dc in next st, dc in each of next 6 sts] around, join with sl st in 3rd ch of beg ch-3. *(165 dc)*

Rnd 14: Ch 3, dc in each st around, join with sl st in 3rd ch of beg ch-3.

Rnd 15: Ch 3, dc in each of next 4 sts, [2 dc in next st, dc in each of next 7 sts] around, join with sl st in 3rd ch of beg ch-3. *(185 dc)*

Rnds 16 & 17: Ch 3, dc in each st around, join with sl st in 3rd ch of beg ch-3.

Rnd 18: Ch 1, sc in each st around, join with sl st in beg sc.

Ruffle

Rnd 19: Ch 3, 2 dc in same st, 3 dc in each of next 3 sts, 2 dc in next st, [3 dc in each of next 4 sts, 2 dc in next st] around, join with sl st in 3rd ch of beg ch-3. *(518 dc)*

Rnd 20: Ch 3, dc in each st around, join with sl st in 3rd ch of beg ch-3. Fasten off.

Rnd 21: Join lavender with sc in first st, [ch 3, sk next st, sc in next st] around, sk last st, ch 1, join with dc in first st forming last ch sp.

Rnd 22: [Ch 4, sl st in 3rd ch from hook, ch 1, sc in next ch sp] around, ending with ch 1, join with sl st in joining dc of last rnd. Fasten off.

Bodice

Row 1: Holding Overskirt on top of Underskirt, working through both thicknesses and working in starting ch on opposite side of row 1, join white with sc in first ch, sc in each ch across, turn. *(17 sc)*

Row 2: Ch 1, sc in each of first 4 sts, 2 sc in next st, sc in each of next 7 sts, 2 sc in next st, sc in each of last 4 sts, turn. *(19 sc)*

Row 3: Ch 1, sc in each st across, turn.

Row 4: Ch 1, sc in each of first 6 sts, 2 sc in each of next 2 sts, sc in each of next 3 sts, 2 sc in each of next 2 sts, sc in each of last 6 sts, turn. *(23 sc)*

Row 5: Ch 1, sc in each st across, turn.

Row 6: Ch 1, sc in each of first 7 sts, 2 sc in each of next 3 sts, sc in each of next 3 sts, 2 sc in each of next 3 sts, sc in each of last 7 sts, turn. *(29 sc)*

Rows 7 & 8: Ch 1, sc in each st across, turn.

Row 9: Ch 1, sc in each of first 8 sts, [**sc dec**—*see Stitch Guide* in next 2 sts] 3 times, sc in next st, [sc dec in next 2 sts] 3 times, sc in each of last 8 sts, turn. *(23 sts)*

Row 10: Ch 1, sc in each st across, turn.

Row 11: Ch 1, sc in each of first 5 sts, for **armhole**, ch 7, sk next st, sc in each of next 11 sts, for **armhole,** ch 7, sk next st, sc in each of last 5 sts, turn.

Row 12: Ch 1, sc in each st and ch across, working ends of row of Bodice, ch 1, sc in each row down first side of back opening on Bodice, sl st evenly around opening on Underskirt only to other side of Bodice opening, sc in each row up 2nd side of back opening, turn, ch 1, sc in each st across to first sl st at waist. Fasten off.

Row 13: With RS of Bodice facing, join lavender with sc in end of row 12, [ch 3, sk next st, sc in next st] across, ending with last sc in opposite end of row 12. Fasten off.

Sleeves

Rnd 1: Join white with sc in skipped st on row 10 of Bodice, ch 1, *(sc, ch 1 counts as first hdc)*, 2 hdc in end of row 11, 2 dc in each of next 7 chs of armhole, 2 hdc in end of row 11, join with sl st in beg ch-1. *(19 sts)*

Rnd 2: Ch 1, 2 sc in first st, hdc in each hdc and dc in each dc around, join with sl st in first sc.

Rnd 3: Ch 1, sc in first st, [dc dec in next 2 sts] around, join with sl st in beg sc.

Rnd 4: Ch 1, sc in each st around, join with sl st in beg sc. Fasten off.

Rnd 5: Join lavender with sc in first st, [ch 3, sc in next st] 9 times, ch 1, join with dc in beg sc forming last ch sp. *(10 sc)*

Rnd 6: [Ch 4, sl st in 3rd ch from hook, ch 1, sc in next ch sp] 9 times, ch 4, sl st in 3rd ch from hook, ch 1, join with sl st in top of joining dc. Fasten off.

Rep on 2nd armhole opening.

Diamond

Row 1: With lavender, ch 2, sc in 2nd

ch from hook, turn. *(1 sc)*

Row 2: Ch 1, 3 sc in sc, turn. *(3 sc)*

Row 3: Ch 1, sc in first st, 2 sc in next st, sc in last st, turn. *(4 sc)*

Row 4: Ch 1, sc in first st, 2 sc in next st, sc in each of last 2 sts, turn. *(5 sc)*

Row 5: Ch 1, sc each of first 2 sts, 2 sc in next st, sc in each of last 2 sts, turn. *(6 sc)*

Row 6: Ch 1, sc in each of first 2 sts, sc dec in next 2 sts, sc in each of last 2 sts, turn. *(5 sc)*

Row 7: Ch 1, sc in first st, sc dec in next 2 sts, sc in each of last 2 sts, turn. *(4 sc)*

Row 8: Ch 1, sc in first st, sc dec in next 2 sts, sc in last st, turn. *(3 sc)*

Row 9: Ch 1, sc dec in first 3 sts. Fasten off. *(1 sc)*

Center and sew Diamond to front of Bodice with lavender.

Hoop

1. For **waistband**, cut a 3⅜-inch piece bias tape, with sewing thread, sew half of a snap to each end with edges tucked under to fit doll's waist snugly *(see Illustration)*.

2. Cut 5 pieces of bias tapes each 9 inches in length *(spokes)* and sew 1 end of each to waistband evenly sp them apart *(see illustration)*.

3. Measure 7-inch length from waistband on each spoke and wrap rem ends evenly sp around metal ring pinning in place to secure *(see illustration)*.

4. Using rem tape to cover ring, fold around ring and sew tog enclosing the wrapped ends of the spokes.

5. Sew lace trim to bottom of wrap on ring.

HAT

Rnd 1: With white *(see Patten Notes)*, ch 2, 5 sc in 2nd ch from hook, join with sl st in beg sc. *(5 sc)*

Rnd 2: Ch 1, 2 sc in each st around, join with sl st in beg sc. *(10 sc)*

Rnd 3: Ch 1, sc in first st, 2 sc in

BARBIE® and associated trademarks are owned by and used with permission from Mattel, Inc. ©2005 Mattel, Inc.

next st, [sc in next st, 2 sc in next st] around, join with sl st in beg sc. *(15 sc)*

Rnd 4: Ch 1, sc in each of first 2 sts, 2 sc in next st, [sc in each of next 2 sts, sc in next st] around, join with sl st in beg sc. *(20 sc)*

Rnd 5: Ch 1, sc in each of first 4 sts, 2 sc in next st, [sc in each of next 4 sts, 2 sc in next st] around, join with sl st in beg sc. *(25 sc)*

Rnds 6–8: Ch 1, sc in each st around, join with sl st in beg sc. At end of last rnd, fasten off.

Rnd 9: Join lavender with sc in first st, [ch 3, sk next st, sc in next st] 12 times, ch 1, join with dc in beg sc forming last ch sp.

Rnd 10: [Ch 4, sc in next ch sp] 12 times, ch 2, join with dc in top of joining dc of last rnd.

Rnd 11: [Ch 5, sl st in 3rd ch from hook, ch 2, sc in next ch sp] 12 times, ch 5, sl st in 3rd ch from hook, ch 2, join with sl st in top of joining dc of last rnd. Fasten off.

PURSE

Rnd 1: Ch 5 *(see Pattern Notes)*, sl st in first ch to form ring, ch 3 *(counts as first dc)*, 14 dc in ring, join with sl st in 3rd ch of beg ch-3. *(15 dc)*

Rnd 2: Ch 3, dc in same st, 2 dc in each st around, join with sl st in 3rd ch of beg ch-3. *(30 dc)*

Rnd 3: Ch 3, dc in same st, dc in next st, [2 dc in next st, dc in next st] around, join with sl st in 3rd ch of beg ch-3. *(45 dc)*

Rnd 4: Ch 3, dc in same st, dc in each of next 2 sts, [2 dc in next st, dc in each of next 2 sts] around, join with sl st in 3rd ch of beg ch-3. *(60 dc)*

Rnd 5: Ch 3, dc in each of next 3 sts, [2 dc in next st, dc in each of next 3 sts] around, join with sl st in 3rd ch of beg ch-3. *(74 dc)*

Rnds 6 & 7: Ch 3, dc in each st around, join with sl st in 3rd ch of beg ch-3.

Rnd 8: Ch 4, sk next st, [tr in next st, ch 1, sk next st] around, join with sl st in 3rd ch of beg ch-4. Fasten off.

Drawstring
Make 2.

Ch 70. Fasten off.

Weave first drawstring from right to left through sts of last rnd on Purse. Tie ends in knot.

Starting on opposite side of Purse, weave 2nd drawstring through last rnd. Tie ends in knot. Pull drawstrings to close Purse.

FINISHING

1. With sewing thread, sew 3 snaps evenly spaced down back opening of Gown.

2. Cut 2 pieces of purple ribbon each 24 inches in length, tie 1 around waist of Gown with bow in front. Tie 2nd piece around crown of Hat and tie bow in back.

3. Cut 10-inch piece purple ribbon, tie in bow and tack to side of Purse with sewing thread.

4. Cut 2 pieces of purple ribbon each 6 inches in length, tie 1 in bow around each Sleeve as shown in photo. ❑❑

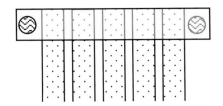

Waistband Illustration

Spoke Illustration

Hearts & Bows Bed Set

Designs by Joyce Bishop

SKILL LEVEL

INTERMEDIATE

FINISHED SIZE
Bed: 6½ x 13½ inches

MATERIALS
- ❑ Fine (sport) weight yarn:
    6 oz/1,050 yds/170g each
    tan and white
- ❑ Crochet cotton size 10:
    60 yds red
    25 yds white
- ❑ Sizes F/5/3.75mm and
    G/6/4mm crochet hooks or size
    needed to obtain gauge
- ❑ Size 7/1.65mm steel
    crochet hook or size
    needed to obtain gauge
- ❑ Tapestry needle
- ❑ Sewing needle
- ❑ Sewing thread to match lace
- ❑ Foam:
    6 x 12½ x 1-inch thick
    (mattress)
    6 x 12½ x 2-inch thick
    (bed base)
- ❑ 5⅝ x 5¾ x ½-inch-thick foam-
    core board (headboard)
- ❑ 1¼ yd 2-inch-wide decorative
    ruffled lace (headboard)
- ❑ 1 yd ⅜-inch-wide picot ribbon
- ❑ Fiberfill

GAUGE
**Size 7 hook and size 10 crochet
cotton:** 9 sc = 1 inch; 11 sc rows =
1 inch
Size F hook and yarn: 5 sc =
1 inch; 5 sc rows = 1 inch
Size G hook and yarn: 7 sc =
2 inches; 4 sc rows = 1 inch

INSTRUCTIONS
BED BASE
Row 1: With size G hook and tan yarn,
ch 41, sc in 2nd ch from hook and
in each ch across, turn. *(40 sc)*

Rows 2–26: Ch 1, sc in each st across, turn.
At end of last row, **do not turn.**

Rnd 27: Working around outer edge,
ch 1, sc in end of each row across,

BARBIE® and associated trademarks are owned by and used with permission from Mattel,
Inc. ©2005 Mattel, Inc.

working in starting ch on opposite
side of row 1, sc in each ch across,
sc in end of each row across, sc in
each st across last row, join with sl
st in beg sc. *(132 sc)*

Rnds 28–31: Ch 1, sc in each st
around, join with sl st in beg sc. At
end of last rnd, turn.

Row 32: For Base bottom, working
in rows, ch 1, sc in each of first
40 sts leaving rem sts unworked,
turn. *(40 sc)*

Rows 33–57: Ch 1, sc in each st across,
turn. At end of last row, fasten off.

Insert foam, fold Base bottom down
to enclose foam and sew matching
edges tog with tan yarn.

Sew 2-inch-wide lace around 2 long
edges and foot of Bed Base with
sewing thread.

HEADBOARD
Side
Make 2.
Row 1: With white yarn and size F
hook, starting at bottom, ch 11, sc
in 2nd ch from hook, sc in each ch
across, turn. *(10 sc)*

Rows 2 & 3: Ch 1, 2 sc in first st, sc
in each st across with 2 sc in last st,
turn. *(14 sc at end of row 3)*

Row 4: Ch 1, sc in each st across,
turn.

Rows 5 & 6: Ch 1, 2 sc in first st, sc
in each st across, turn. *(16 sc at end
of row 6)*

Row 7: Ch 1, 2 sc in first st, sc in
each st across with 2 sc in last st,
turn. *(18 sc)*

Row 8: Ch 1, sc in each st across,
turn.

Row 9: Ch 1, 2 sc in first st, sc in each st across with 2 sc in last st, turn. *(20 sc)*

Rows 10 & 11: Ch 1, 2 sc in first st, sc in each st across, turn. *(22 sc at end of row 11)*

Rows 12 & 13: Ch 1, 2 sc in first st, sc in each st across with 2 sc in last st, turn. *(26 sc at end of row 13)*

Rows 14 & 15: Ch 1, sc in each st across, turn.

Row 16: Ch 1, 2 sc in first st, sc in each st across with 2 sc in last st, turn. *(28 sc)*

Rows 17 & 18: Ch 1, sc in each st across, turn.

Rows 19–22: Ch 1, 2 sc in first st, sc in each st across, turn. *(32 sc at end of row 22)*

Rows 23–26: Ch 1, sc in each st across, turn.

Row 27: Ch 1, sk first st, sc in each st across to last 2 sts, sk next st, sc in last st, turn. *(30 sc)*

Rows 28: Ch 1, sc in each st across, turn.

Row 29: Ch 1, sk first st, sc in each st across to last 2 sts, sk next st, sc in last st, turn. *(28 sc)*

First Side

Row 30: Ch 1, sk first st, sc in each of next 11 sts, sk next st, sc in next st, leaving last 14 sts unworked, turn. *(12 sc)*

Rows 31–34: Ch 1, sk first st, sc in each st across to last 2 sts, sk next st, sc in last st, turn. At end of last row, fasten off. *(4 sc)*

Second Side

Row 30: Join white yarn with sc in next unworked st on row 29, sk next st, sc in each of next 10 sts, sk next st, sc in last st, turn. *(12 sc)*

Rows 31–34: Ch 1, sk first st, sc in each st across to last 2 sts, sk next st, sc in last st, turn. At end of last row, fasten off. *(4 sc)*

Using 1 crocheted piece as pattern, cut heart shape from ½-inch-thick foam-core board ¼-inch shorter on all edges.

Assembly

Rnd 1: Hold Headboard Sides tog, matching sts and ends of rows, working through both thicknesses and inserting foam before closing, with size F hook, join white yarn with sc in any st, sc in each st and in end of each row around with 3 sc in each end of row 1, join with sl st in beg sc. Fasten off.

Rnd 2: With size 7 hook and red crochet cotton, working around **posts** *(see Stitch Guide)* below tops of each sc on rnd 1, join with sl st around any post, sl st around each post around, join with sl st in beg sl st. Fasten off.

Beg and ending at each end of row 1, at bottom of assembled Headboard, sew 1½-inch-wide lace around outer edge of Headboard with sewing thread.

Cut 12-inch length of ribbon, tie in bow and tack to center front of Headboard.

With white yarn, sew bottom of Headboard centered to head of Bed Base with RS of Headboard facing forward.

MATTRESS

Row 1: With white yarn and size F hook, ch 51, sc in 2nd ch from hook and in each ch across, turn. *(50 sc)*

Rows 2–30: Ch 1, sc in each st across, turn. At end of last row, **do not turn.**

Rnd 31: Working around outer edge, ch 1, sc in end of each row across, working in starting ch on opposite side of row 1, sc in each ch across, sc in end of each row across, sc in each st across last row, join with sl st in beg sc. *(160 sc)*

Rnds 32–35: Ch 1, sc in each st around, join. At end of last rnd, turn.

Mattress Bottom

Row 36: Ch 1, sc in each of first 50 sts leaving rem sts unworked, turn.

Rows 37–65: Ch 1, sc in each st across, turn. At end of last row, fasten off.

Insert foam, fold mattress bottom down to enclose foam and sew matching edges tog with white yarn.

Place on top of Bed Base.

COVERLET

Row 1: With size F hook and white yarn, ch 27, sc in 2nd ch from hook and in each ch across, turn. *(26 sc)*

Rows 2–58: Ch 1, sc in each st across, turn. At end of last row, do not turn.

Row 59: Ch 1, sc in end of each row across, working in starting ch on opposite side of row 1, 2 sc in first ch, sc in each ch across with 2 sc in last ch, sc in end of each row across, turn.

Row 60: Working in **front lps** *(see Stitch Guide)*, ch 1, sc in each st across last row, turn.

Rows 61–65: Ch 1, sc in each st across, turn.

Row 66: Ch 1, sc in first st, ch 3, dc in front lp and left bar of sc just made, [sk next 2 sts, sc in next st, ch 3, dc in front lp and left bar of sc just made] across, sc in last st. Fasten off.

Row 67: With size 7 hook and red crochet cotton, working around post of sts below unworked back lp of row 59, join with sl st around first st, sl st in each st across. Fasten off.

Cut rem ribbon in half, tie each in bow and sew 1 to each bottom corner of Coverlet with sewing thread as shown in photo.

Place Coverlet over Mattress.

BOLSTER
End
Make 2.

Row 1: With size F hook and white yarn ch 2, 6 sc in 2nd ch from hook, join with sl st in beg sc. *(6 sc)*

Rnd 2: Ch 1, 2 sc in first st, 2 sc in each st around, join with sl st in beg sc. *(12 sc)*

Rnd 3: Ch 1, sc in first st, 2 sc in next st, [sc in next st, 2 sc in next st] around, join with sl st in beg sc. *(18 sc)*

Rnd 4: Ch 1, sc in each of first 2 sts, 2 sc in next st, [sc in each of next 2 sts, 2 sc in next st] around, join with sl st in beg sc. Fasten off. *(24 sc)*

Side

Row 1: With white yarn and size F hook, ch 25, sc in 2nd ch from hook and in each ch across, turn. *(24 sc)*

Rows 2–30: Ch 1, sc in each st across, turn. At end of last row, fasten off.

Matching ends of rows, sew long edges of side tog with white yarn. Working in back lps of End, sew End pieces to each open end of Side.

Edging

Rnd 1: Working in rem front lps of End with Side pointing away from you, with size F hook, join white yarn with sc in any st, ch 3, dc in front lp and left bar of sc just made, sk next st, [sc in next st, ch 3, dc in front lp and left bar of sc just made] around, join with sl st in beg sc, **turn.** Fasten off.

Rnd 2: Working around post of sts, with size 7 hook and red crochet cotton, join with sl st around first st, sl st around each st around, join with sl st in beg sl st. Fasten off.

Rep on 2nd End. Place Bolster in front of Headboard.

SMALL HEART PILLOW
Side
Make 2.
Row 1: With size 7 hook and red crochet cotton, ch 2, 3 sc in 2nd ch from hook, turn. *(3 sc)*

Row 2: Ch 1, sc in first st, 2 sc in next st, sc in last st, turn. *(4 sc)*

Rows 3 & 4: Ch 1, 2 sc in first st, sc in each st across with 2 sc in last st, turn. *(8 sc at end of row 4)*

Row 5: Ch 1, sc in each st across, turn.

Rows 6 & 7: Ch 1, 2 sc in first st, sc in each st across with 2 sc in last st, turn. *(12 sc at end of row 7)*

Row 8: Ch 1, sc in each st across, turn.

Rows 9 & 10: Ch 1, 2 sc in first st, sc in each st across with 2 sc in last st, turn. *(16 sc at end of row 10)*

Rows 11–13: Ch 1, sc in each st across, turn.

Row 14: Ch 1, sk first st, sc in each st across to last 2 sts, sk next st, sc in last st, turn. *(14 sc)*

Row 15: Ch 1, sc in first st, hdc in each of next 5 sts, sl st in each of next 2 sts, hdc in each of next 5 sts, sc in last st, turn.

First Side
Row 16: Ch 1, sc in first st, hdc in each of next 3 sts, sc in next st, sl st in next st leaving rem sts unworked, turn.

Row 17: Ch 1, sk first sl st, sc in next st, hdc in each of next 2 sts, sc in next st, sl st in next st. Fasten off.

Second Side
Row 16: Sk next 2 unworked sts on row 15, join red Crochet cotton with sc

in next st, hdc in each of next 3 sts, sc in next st, sl st in last st, turn.

Row 17: Ch 1, sk first sl st, sc in next st, hdc in each of next 2 sts, sc in next st, sl st in next st. Fasten off.

Edging
Rnd 1: With RS of Pillow Sides tog, working around outer edge in sts, in ends of rows and in starting ch on opposite side of row 1, with size 7 hook, join red Crochet cotton with sc in any st, sc in each st around with 3 sc in bottom tip of Heart, stuffing before closing, join with sl st in beg sc. Fasten off.

Rnd 2: Join white Crochet cotton with sc in first st, ch 2, 2 dc in same st, sc in next st, [3 dc in next st, sc in next st] around, join with sl st in beg sc. Fasten off.

MEDIUM HEART PILLOW
Side
Make 2.
Row 1: With size 7 hook and white crochet cotton, ch 2, 3 sc in 2nd ch from hook, turn. *(3 sc)*

Row 2: Ch 1, sc in first st, 2 sc in next st, sc in last st, turn. *(4 sc)*

Rows 3 & 4: Ch 1, 2 sc in first st, sc in each st across with 2 sc in last st, turn. *(8 sc at end of row 4)*

Row 5: Ch 1, sc in each st across, turn.

Rows 6 & 7: Ch 1, 2 sc in first st, sc in each st across with 2 sc in last st, turn. *(12 sc at end of row 7)*

Row 8: Ch 1, sc in each st across, turn.

Rows 9 & 10: Ch 1, 2 sc in first st, sc in each st across with 2 sc in last st, turn. *(16 sc at end of row 10)*

Row 11: Ch 1, sc in each st across, turn.

Rows 12 & 13: Ch 1, 2 sc in first st, sc in each st across with 2 sc in last st, turn. *(20 sc at end of row 13)*

Rows 14–17: Ch 1, sc in each st across, turn.

Row 18: Ch 1, sc in first st, hdc in each of next 7 sts, sc in next st, sl st in each of next 2 sts, sc in next sts, hdc in each of next 7 sts, sc in last st, turn.

First Side
Row 19: Ch 1, sk first st, sc in next st,

hdc in each of next 5 sts, sk next st, sc in next st, sl st in next st leaving rem sts unworked, turn.

Row 20: Ch 1, sk first st, sc in next st, hdc in each of next 3 sts, sk next st, sc in next st, sl st in next st. Fasten off.

Second Side
Row 19: Sk next unworked st on row 18, join red Crochet cotton with sc in next st, sk next st, hdc in each of next 5 sts, sp in next st, sc in last st, turn.

Row 20: Ch 1, sk first st, sc in next st, hdc in each of next 3 sts, sk next st, sc in next st, sl st in next st on row 18. Fasten off.

Edging
Rnd 1: With RS of Pillow Sides tog, working around outer edge in sts, ends of rows and in starting ch on opposite side of row 1, with size 7 hook, join white Crochet cotton with sc in any st, sc in each st around with 3 sc in bottom tip of Heart, stuffing before closing, join with sl st in beg sc. Fasten off.

Rnd 2: Join red Crochet cotton with sc in first st, ch 2, 2 dc in same st, sc in next st, [3 dc in next st, sc in next st] around, join with sl st in beg sc. Fasten off.

LARGE HEART PILLOW
Side
Make 2.
Row 1: With size 7 hook and red crochet cotton, ch 3, sc in 2nd ch from hook and in last ch, turn. *(2 sc)*

Row 2: Ch 1, 2 sc in first st, 2 sc in last st, turn. *(4 sc)*

Rows 3–5: Ch 1, 2 sc in first st, sc in each st across with 2 sc in last st, turn. *(10 sc at end of row 5)*

Row 6: Ch 1, 3 sc in first st, sc in each st across with 3 sc in last st, turn. *(14 sc)*

Row 7: Ch 1, sc in each st across, turn.

Row 8: Ch 1, 3 sc in first st, sc in each st across with 3 sc in last st, turn. *(18 sc)*

Rows 9 & 10: Ch 1, 2 sc in first st, sc in each sc across, turn. *(20 sc at end of row 10)*

Row 11: Ch 1, 3 sc in first st, sc in

each st across with 3 sc in last st, turn. *(24 sc)*

Row 12: Ch 1, sc in each st across, turn.

Row 13: Ch 1, 3 sc in first st, sc in each st across with 3 sc in last st, turn. *(28 sc)*

Rows 14–19: Ch 1, sc in each st across, turn.

Rows 20–25: Ch 1, sk first st, sc in each st across, turn. *(22 sc at end of row 25)*

First Side

Row 26: Ch 1, sk first st, sc in each of next 10 sts leaving rem sts unworked, turn.

Rows 27 & 28: Ch 1, sk first st, sc in each st across, turn. *(8 sc at end of row 28)*

Rows 29 & 30: Ch 1, sk first st, sc in each st across to last 2 sts, sk next st, sc in last st, turn. At end of last row, fasten off. *(4 sc)*

Second Side

Row 26: Join red Crochet cotton with sc in next unworked st on row 25, sk next st, sc in each of last 9 sts, turn.

Rows 27 & 28: Ch 1, sk first st, sc in each st across, turn. *(8 sc at end of row 28)*

Rows 29 & 30: Ch 1, sk first st, sc in each st across to last 2 sts, sk next st, sc in last st, turn. At end of last row, fasten off. *(4 sc)*

Assembly

With WS of Pillow Sides held tog, working around outer edge in ends of rows, in sts and in starting ch on opposite side of row 1, with size 7 hook, join red Crochet cotton with sc in any st, sc in each st around with 3 sc in tip of Heart, stuffing before closing, join with sl st in beg sc. Fasten off.

Arrange 3 Heart Pillows in front of Bolster on Bed. ❏❏

Country Woven Rug

Design by Debra Woodard

SKILL LEVEL

EASY

FINISHED SIZE

4½ x 5¼ inches, without fringe

MATERIALS

- ❑ Crochet cotton size 10:
   150 yds ecru
   50 yds blue
- ❑ Size 5/1.90mm steel crochet hook or size needed to obtain gauge
- ❑ Embroidery needle

GAUGE

7 hdc = 1 inch; 6 hdc rows = 1 inch

INSTRUCTIONS

RUG

Row 1: With ecru, ch 36, hdc in 3rd ch from hook *(first 2 chs count as first dc)*, hdc in each ch across, turn. *(35 hdc)*

Rows 2–25: Ch 2, hdc in each st across, turn.

Border

Rnd 26: Working around entire outer edge, ch 2, 2 hdc in same st, hdc in each st across to last st, 3 hdc in last st, *hdc in end of first row, [2 hdc in end of next row, hdc in end of next row] across*, working in rem lps of starting ch on opposite side of row 1, 3 hdc in first ch, hdc in each ch across to last ch, 3 hdc in last ch, rep between *, join with sl st in 2nd ch of beg ch-2. Fasten off.

Cross-stitch over hdc

Horizontal Weaving

Row 1: With embroidery needle threaded with a 10-inch strand of blue, leaving a 2-inch end at each end, weave running sts *(see illustration)* over top of 1 st and under top of next st across row.

Row 2: With another 10-inch strand

Running Stitch

of blue, reversing weaving from first row, weave running sts under top of 1 st and over top of next st across 2nd row.

Next rows: Work weaving rows 1 and 2 alternately across all rows.

Vertical Weaving

Row 3: Working between first and 2nd sts of each row, leaving 2-inch end at each end, weave a 10-inch strand of blue over and under across all rows.

Row 4: Reversing weaving sts from last row, weave 10-inch strand of thread under and over between 2nd and 3rd sts of all rows.

Next rows: Work weaving rows 3 and 4 alternately across all rows.

Fringe

Hold ends of 2 strands tog and tie in knot.

Place Fringe around entire outer edge.

Heart

Following graph using cross-st *(see illustration)*, embroider Heart in center of Rug, using a single strand of blue. ❑❑

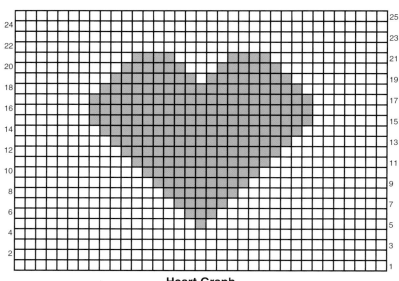

Heart Graph

A Day at the Beach

Designs by Deborah Levy-Hamburg

FINISHED SIZES
Bag: 2¼ square, excluding handles
Towel: 5 x 10 inches, excluding fringe
Hat: 2¾ inches across

MATERIALS
❑ Pearl cotton size 8:
   30 yds medium teal
   small amount each of yellow,
   light green and orange
❑ Pearl cotton size 5:
   106 yds medium teal
   80 yds light green
❑ Size 7/1.65mm steel
   crochet hook or size
   needed to obtain gauges
❑ Sewing needle
❑ White sewing thread
❑ 2mm beads:
   1 black seed
   3 white pearl

GAUGE
Bag: 10 hdc sts = 1 inch; 8 hdc
rows = 1 inch
Towel: 5 V-sts and 4 ch-1 sps =
2 inches; 2 V-sts and 2 shell rows =
1 inch
Hat: Rnd 1 = 1¼ inches across

PATTERN NOTES
Bag is made with size 8 pearl cotton.

Blanket and Hat are made with size
5 pearl cotton.

SPECIAL STITCHES
V-stitch (V-st): (Dc, ch 1, dc).

Shell: (2 dc, ch 1, 2 dc).

Beginning shell (beg shell): (Ch
3, dc, ch 1, 2 dc).

Treble cluster (tr cl): *Yo twice,
insert hook in st or sp, yo, pull lp
through, [yo, pull through 2 lps
on hook] twice leaving last lps on
hook, working in same st or sp, rep

BARBIE® and associated trademarks are owned by and used with permission from Mattel, Inc. ©2005 Mattel, Inc.

from * number of times needed for
number of tr in cl, yo, pull through
all lps on hook.

INSTRUCTIONS
BAG
First Side
Row 1: With medium teal, ch 25, hdc
in 2nd ch from hook, hdc in each ch
across, turn. *(24 hdc)*
Rows 2–5: Ch 1, hdc in first st, hdc
in each st across, turn.
Row 6: Ch 2, dc in each st across,
turn.
Rows 7–14: Ch 1, hdc in first st, hdc
in each st across, turn.
Row 15: Ch 2, dc in each st across,
turn.
Row 16: Ch 1, hdc in first st, hdc in
each st across, turn.

Row 17: Sl st in each of first 7 sts, for
Handle, ch 12, sk next 10 sts, sl st
in next st, **turn,** ch 1, working in
chs of Handle, sl st in each ch across,
turn, ch 1, working behind Handle,
sl st in each of 10 sk sts, sl st in each
of rem 6 sts. Fasten off.

Second Side
Row 18: Working on opposite
side of starting ch on row 1, join
medium teal with sl st in first ch, ch
1, hdc in same ch, hdc in each ch
across, turn.
Rows 19–34: Rep rows 2–17 of First
Side.

FISH
Head
Row 1: With light green, ch 8, sc in

2nd ch from hook, and in each ch across, turn. *(7 sc)*

Row 2: Ch 1, sc in each st across, turn.

Bottom of Mouth
Row 3: Ch 1, **sc dec** *(see Stitch Guide)* in first 2 sts, sc in next st leaving last 4 sts unworked, turn. *(2 sc)*

Row 4: Ch 1, sc in first st, sc in last st, turn.

Row 5: Ch 1, sc dec in next 2 sts, **do not turn.** Fasten off.

Top of Mouth
Row 3: Sk next unworked st on row 2, join light green with sc in next st, sc dec in last 2 sts, turn. *(2 sc)*

Row 4: Ch 1, sc in first st, sc in last st, turn.

Row 5: Ch 1, sc dec in next 2 sts, **do not turn.** Fasten off.

Body
Row 6: Working on opposite side of starting ch on row 1, join yellow with sc in first ch, sc in same ch, sc in each of next 5 chs, 2 sc in last ch, turn. *(9 sc)*

Rows 7–9: Ch 1, sc in each st across, turn. At end of last row, fasten off.

Row 10: Join orange with sc in first st, sc in each st across, turn.

First Fin
Row 11: Ch 1, sc in first st, sc in next st leaving last 7 sts unworked, turn.

Row 12: Ch 1, sc dec in next 2 sts, turn. Fasten off.

Tail
Row 11: Sk next unworked st on row 10, join orange with sc in next st, sc in each of next 2 sts leaving last 3 sts unworked, turn. *(3 sc)*

Row 12: Ch 1, sc in each st across, turn.

Row 13: Ch 1, 2 sc in first st, sl st in next st, 2 sc in last st, turn. *(5 sc)*

Rows 14 & 15: Ch 1, 2 sc in first st, sl st in each st across to last st, 2 sc

in last st, turn. At end of last row, **do not turn.** Fasten off. *(9 sc)*

Second Fin
Row 11: Join orange with sc in next unworked st on row 10, sc in each of last 2 sts, turn. *(3 sc)*

Row 12: Ch 1, sc in first st, sc dec in last 2 sts, turn. *(2 sc)*

Row 13: Ch 1, sc dec in next 2 sts. Fasten off.

Fold Bag in half and sew side edges tog.

For **eye**, sew black bead to row 2 at top of Head.

Sew Fish to Bag as shown in photo.

For **bubbles**, sew 3 pearl beads to Bag as shown in photo.

TOWEL
Row 1: With medium teal, ch 72, working in 1 lp of ch only, dc in 4th ch from hook and in each ch across, turn. *(70 dc)*

Row 2: Ch 3 *(counts as first dc)*, sk first 2 sts, **V-st** *(see Special Stitches)* in next st, [sk next 2 sts, V-st in next st] 21 times, sk next 2 sts, dc in last st, turn. *(22 V-sts)*

Row 3: Ch 3, **shell** *(see Special Stitches)* in ch sp of first V-st, shell in ch sp of each V-st across, dc in last st, turn. *(22 shells)*

Row 4: Ch 3, V-st in ch sp of each shell across, dc in last st, turn. Fasten off.

Row 5: Join light green with sl st in first st, ch 3, shell in each V-st across, dc in last st, turn.

Row 6: Ch 3, V-st in each shell across, dc in last st, turn.

Row 7: Ch 3, shell in each V-st across, dc in last st, turn.

Row 8: Ch 3, V-st in each shell across, dc in last st, turn. Fasten off.

Rows 9–12: With medium teal, rep rows 5–8.

Rows 13–16: Rep rows 5–8.

Rows 17–19: With medium teal, rep rows 5–7.

Row 20: Ch 3, 2 dc in sp before first shell, dc in first shell, [2 dc in sp

between next 2 shells, dc in shell] across, 2 dc in sp after last shell, dc in last st. Fasten off.

Fringe
Cut 1 strand 2¼ inches long. Fold in half, insert hook in st, pull fold through st, pull ends through fold, tighten.

With matching colors, evenly sp 42 Fringe across ends of rows at each end of Towel.

HAT
Rnd 1: With medium teal, ch 6, sl st in first ch to form ring, ch 3, **2-tr cl** *(see Special Stitches)* in ring, ch 3, [3-tr cl in ring, ch 3) 6 times. Fasten off. *(7 tr cls, 7 ch-3 sps)*

Rnd 2: Join light green with sl st in any ch-3 sp, **beg shell** *(see Special Stitches)* in same ch sp, shell in each ch sp around, join with sl st in 3rd ch of beg ch-3. *(7 shells)*

Rnd 3: Sl st back in sp between joined shells, ch 4 *(counts as first dc and ch 1)*, dc in same sp, V-st in ch sp of first shell, [V-st in sp between next 2 shells, V-st in ch sp of next shell] around, join with sl st in 3rd ch of beg ch-4. Fasten off. *(14 V-sts)*

Rnd 4: Join medium teal with sl st in ch-1 sp of any V-st between shells, beg shell in same sp, [sk next V-st, shell in ch sp of next V-st] around, sk last V-st, join with sl st in 3rd ch of beg ch-3. *(7 shells)*

Rnd 5: Sl st back in sp between joined shell, ch 4, dc in same sp, V-st in ch sp of first shell, [V-st in sp between next 2 shells, V-st in ch sp of next shell] around, join with sl st in 3rd ch of beg ch-4. *(14 V-sts)*

Rnd 6: Sl st in ch-1 sp of joined V-st, ch 4, 6 tr in same ch sp, dc in ch sp of next V-st, [7 tr in ch sp of next V-st, dc in ch sp of next V-st] around, join with sl st in 3rd ch of beg ch-4. Fasten off.

Rnd 7: Join light green with sc in any sp between dc and tr, sc in each sp around, join with sl st in beg sc. Fasten off. ❏❏

Grandma's Feather Bed

Design by Joyce Bishop

SKILL LEVEL

INTERMEDIATE

FINISHED SIZE
Fits 11½-inch fashion doll

MATERIALS
- ❑ Medium (worsted) weight yarn:
  10 oz/500 yds/283g burgundy
  ½ oz/25 yds/14g pink
  Small amount each of blue
  and white
- ❑ Fine (sport) weight yarn:
  4 oz/680 yds/113g white
  2 oz/340 yds/57g pink
- ❑ Sizes D/3/3.25mm and
  F/5/3.75mm crochet hooks or
  sizes needed to obtain gauge
- ❑ Tapestry needle
- ❑ Sewing needle
- ❑ Sewing thread
- ❑ 6¼ x 12 x 3½-inch piece foam
- ❑ Plastic foam board:
  6¼ x 4-inch piece
  (footboard)
  6¼ x 6⅞-inch piece
  (headboard)
- ❑ 2 pieces of 3-inch-wide gathered lace, each 14 inches long
- ❑ 20-inch piece 1½-inch-wide
  gathered lace
- ❑ Polyester fiberfill

GAUGE
Size D hook and sport yarn: Each
Motif is 1½ inches across
Size F hook and worsted yarn:
4 sc = 1 inch; 9 sc rows = 2 inches;
2 dc rows = 1 inch

INSTRUCTIONS
BED
Headboard Front
Row 1: With burgundy worsted yarn
and size F hook, ch 27, sc in 2nd ch
from hook and in each ch across,
turn. *(26 sc)*

Rows 2–50: Ch 1, sc in each st across,
turn. At end of last row, fasten off.

Headboard Back
Row 1: With burgundy worsted yarn

BARBIE® and associated trademarks are owned by and used with permission from Mattel, Inc. ©2005 Mattel, Inc.

and size F hook, ch 27, sc in 2nd ch
from hook and in each ch across,
turn. *(26 sc)*

Rows 2–34: Ch 1, sc in each st across,
turn. At end of last row, fasten off.

Footboard Front
Row 1: With burgundy worsted yarn
and size F hook, ch 27, sc in 2nd ch
from hook and in each ch across,
turn. *(26 sc)*

Rows 2–32: Ch 1, sc in each st across,
turn. At end of last row, fasten off.

Footboard Back
Row 1: With burgundy worsted yarn

and size F hook, ch 27, sc in 2nd ch
from hook and in each ch across,
turn. *(26 sc)*

Rows 2–19: Ch 1, sc in each st across,
turn. At end of last row, fasten off.

Head/Footboard End
Make 4.

With burgundy worsted yarn and size
F hook, ch 3, 11 hdc in 3rd ch from
hook, join with sl st in top of ch 2.
Fasten off.

Head/Footboard Knob
Make 4.

With burgundy worsted yarn and size

F hook, ch 2, 7 sc in 2nd ch from hook, join with sl st in top of beg sc. Leaving long end, fasten off.

Weave end through **back lps** (*see Stitch Guide*) and pull tight. Secure end.

Head/Footboard Edge
Make 4.
With burgundy worsted yarn and size F hook, ch 35, hdc in **back bar** (*see illustration*) of 3rd ch and hdc in back bar of each ch across to last ch, sc in last ch. Fasten off.

Back Bar of Chain

Top & Bottom
Row 1: With burgundy worsted yarn and size F hook, ch 28, dc in 3rd ch from hook and in each ch across, turn. (*26 dc*)

Rows 2–24: Ch 3 (*counts as first dc*), dc in each st across, turn. At end of last row, fasten off.

End
Make 2.
Row 1: With burgundy worsted yarn and size F hook, ch 27, sc in 2nd ch from hook and in each ch across, turn. (*26 sc*)

Rows 2–16: Ch 1, sc in each st across, turn. At end of last row, fasten off.

Side
Make 2.
Row 1: With burgundy worsted yarn and size F hook, ch 49, sc in 2nd ch from hook and in each ch across, turn. (*48 sc*)

Rows 2–16: Ch 1, sc in each st across, turn. At end of last row, fasten off.

Assembly
1. For Headboard, working in back lps of Edges and matching bottom edges, sew Edges to Front leaving 16 rows at top of Front unsewn (*see illustration*). Sew Edges to Back. Tack top edge of Front to top edge of Back forming a tube. Stuff tube with fiberfill.

2. Sew a Knob to center of Ends. Sew 1 End to each end of roll.

3. Insert foam board inside lower por-

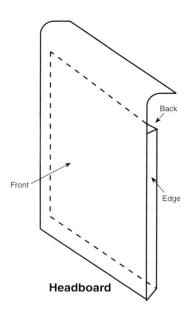

Headboard

tion of Headboard and sew bottom closed.

4. Rep steps 1–3 with Footboard and rem pieces.

5. For mattress, sew Sides to Ends and sew to Top (*see illustration*). Sew Bottom to Sides and Ends inserting foam pieces before closing.

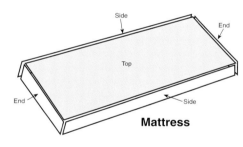

Mattress

6. Tack Footboard Front to 1 End and Headboard to other End.

7. Sew a ¼-inch hem in each end of each 14-inch piece of lace. Tack 1 piece to each Side of Bed ½-inch from top edge.

PILLOW SHAM
Side
Make 2.
Row 1: With pink worsted yarn and size F hook, ch 27, sc in 2nd ch from hook and in each ch across, turn. (*26 sc*)

Rows 2–10: Ch 1, sc in each st across, turn. At end of last row, fasten off.

Using sewing thread and needle, sew ends of 1½-inch-wide lace tog. Sew Sides tog with edge of lace between, tucking lace at corner for fullness and stuffing before closing.

SMALL PILLOW
Front
Make 2.
Rnd 1: With pink worsted yarn and size F hook, ch 4, 2 dc in 4th ch from hook, (ch 2, 3 dc) 3 times in same ch, join with sl st in 4th ch of beg ch-4. Fasten off.

Rnd 2: Join white worsted yarn with sl st in any ch sp, (ch 3, 2 dc, ch 1, 3 dc) in same ch sp, (3 dc, ch 1, 3 dc) in each ch sp around, join with sl st in 3rd ch of beg ch-3. Fasten off.

Back
Make 2.
Rnd 1: With white worsted yarn and size F hook, ch 4, 11 dc in 4th ch from hook (*first 3 chs count as first dc*), join with sl st in 4th ch.

Rnd 2: Ch 3, dc in next st, 5 dc in next st, [dc in each of next 2 sts, 5 dc in next st] around, join with sl st in 3rd ch of beg ch-3. Fasten off.

For each Pillow, sew 1 Front and Back WS tog, stuffing before closing.

QUILT
Motif
Make 46.
Rnd 1: With pink sport yarn and size D hook, ch 4, 2 dc in 4th ch from hook (*first 3 chs count as first dc*), (ch 2, 3 dc) 3 times in same ch, join with sl st in 4th ch of beg ch-4. Fasten off.

Rnd 2: Join white sport yarn with sl st in any ch sp, (ch 3, 2 dc, ch 2, 3 dc) in same ch sp, (3 dc, ch 2, 3 dc) in each ch sp around, join with sl st in 3rd ch of beg ch-3. Fasten off.

Sew Motifs tog according to illustration. Sew edges of corner Motifs at bottom tog according to arrows to form corners.

RUG
Rnd 1: With burgundy worsted yarn and size F hook, ch 4, 2 sc in 2nd ch from hook, sc in next ch, 3 sc in last ch, working on opposite side of starting ch, sc in next ch, 2 sc in next ch, join with sl st in beg sc. Fasten off. (*9 sc*)

Rnd 2: Join blue worsted yarn with sc in first st, sc in same st, sc in each of next 3 sts, 4 sc in next st, sc in each of next 3 sts, 2 sc in next st, join with

Top

Quilt

sl st in beg sc. Fasten off. *(14 sc)*

Rnd 3: Join burgundy worsted yarn with sc in first st, 2 sc in next st, sc in each of next 3 sts, 2 sc in next st, sc in each of next 2 sts, 2 sc in next st, sc in each of next 3 sts, 2 sc in next st, sc in last st, join with sl st in beg sc. Fasten off.

Rnd 4: Join white worsted yarn with sc in first st, 2 sc in next st, sc in each of next 5 sts, 2 sc in next st, sc in each of next 2 sts, 2 sc in next st, sc in each of next 5 sts, 2 sc in next st, sc in last st, join with sl st in beg sc. Fasten off.

Rnd 5: Join burgundy worsted yarn with sc in first st, sc in same st, sc in next st, 2 sc in next st, sc in each of next 5 sts, 2 sc in next st, sc in next st, 2 sc in each of next 2 sts, sc in next st, 2 sc in next st, sc in each of next 5 sts, 2 sc in next st, sc in next st, 2 sc in last st, join with sl st in beg sc. Fasten off.

Rnd 6: Join pink worsted yarn with sc in first st, 2 sc in each of next 2 sts, sc in each of next 9 sts, 2 sc in each of next 2 sts, sc in each of next 2 sts, 2 sc in each of next 2 sts, sc in each of next 9 sts, 2 sc in each of next 2 sts, sc in last st, join with sl st in beg sc. Fasten off.

Rnd 7: Join white worsted yarn with sc in first st, sc in same st, sc in each of next 2 sts, 2 sc in next st, sc in each of next 11 sts, [2 sc in next st, sc in each of next 2 sts, 2 sc in next st] twice, sc in each of next 11 sts, 2 sc in next st, sc in each of next 2 sts, 2 sc in last st, join with sl st in beg sc. Fasten off.

Rnd 8: Join blue worsted yarn with sc in first st, sc in each st around, join with sl st in beg sc. Fasten off.

Rnd 9: Join burgundy worsted with sc in first st, sc in each of next 2 sts, 2 sc in next st, sc in next st, 2 sc in next st, sc in each of next 11 sts, 2 sc in next st, sc in next st, 2 sc in next st, sc in each of next 6 sts, 2 sc in next st, sc in next st, 2 sc in next st, sc in each of next 11 sts, 2 sc in next st, sc in next st, 2 sc in next st, sc in each of last 3 sts, join with sl st in beg sc. Fasten off.

Rnd 10: Join pink worsted yarn with sc in first st, *[sc in each of next 2 sts, 2 sc in next st] twice, sc in each of next 13 sts, 2 sc in next st, sc in each of next 2 sts, 2 sc in next st*, sc in each of next 4 sts, rep between *, sc in each of last 3 sts, join with sl st in beg sc. Fasten off.

Rnd 11: Join burgundy worsted yarn with sc in first st, working from left to right, **reverse sc** *(see illustration)* around, join with sl st in beg sc. Fasten off. ❑❑

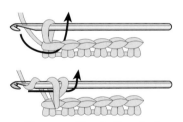

Reverse Single Crochet

Springtime Sundress

Designs by Lucille LaFlamme

SKILL LEVEL
INTERMEDIATE

FINISHED SIZE
Fits 11½-inch fashion doll

MATERIALS
- ❑ Crochet cotton size 10:
  - 1 ball yellow
  - ½ ball dark pink
  - ½ ball light green
  - small amount light blue
- ❑ Size 7/1.65mm steel crochet hook or size needed to obtain gauge
- ❑ Embroidery needle
- ❑ 3 small snaps
- ❑ 20 inches of ½-inch-wide pink ribbon

GAUGE
10 dc, = 1 inch; 4 dc rows = 1 inch

PATTERN NOTE
Dress is worked in 1 piece from the neck down.

SPECIAL STITCH
Treble crochet decrease (tr dec): Holding back last lp on each tr on hook, work tr in each specified st, yo, pull through all lps on hook.

INSTRUCTIONS
DRESS
Bodice

Row 1: Starting at neck edge, with yellow, ch 25 loosely, sc in 2nd ch from hook, [ch 1, sc in next ch] across, turn. *(24 sc)*

Row 2: Ch 1, sc in first sc, [sc in next ch-1 sp, sc in next sc] across, turn. *(70 sc)*

Row 3: Ch 3, dc in same st, [sk next 2 sc, 3 dc in next sc] across, ending with sk 2 sc, 2 dc in last sc, turn. *(70 dc)*

Row 4: Ch 3, dc in next dc, [ch 1, 3 dc in center dc of next 3-dc group] across, ch 1, dc in each of last 2 dc, turn.

Row 5: Ch 3, dc in next dc, [3 dc in next ch-1 sp, dc in center dc of next 3-dc group] across, 3 dc in

last ch-1 sp, dc in each of last 2 dc, turn. *(95 dc)*

Row 6: Ch 3, dc in each dc across, turn.

Row 7: Ch 3, dc in each of next 9 dc, sk next 21 dc for armhole, [dc in each of next 4 dc, sk next dc] 6 times, dc in each of next 4 dc, sk next 21 dc for armhole, dc in each of last 9 dc, turn. *(47 dc)*

Row 8: Ch 3, dc in each of next 4 dc,

[sk next dc, dc in each of next 3 dc] 9 times, sk next dc, dc in each of last 5 dc, turn. *(37 dc)*

Row 9: Ch 3, dc in each of next 4 dc, [sk next dc, dc in each of next 5 dc] 4 times, sk next dc, dc in each of last 7 dc, turn. *(32 dc)*

Row 10: Ch 3, dc in each dc across, turn.

Skirt

Row 1: Ch 5 *(counts as first tr and ch 1)*, tr in same dc, (ch 1, tr) twice in each dc across, turn. *(64 tr)*

Row 2: Ch 4 *(counts as first tr)*, tr in next ch-1 sp, [ch 1, 2 tr in next ch-1 sp] across to last ch-1 sp, tr in last ch-1 sp, tr in 4th ch of beg ch-5 of row 1, turn. *(126 tr)*

Rnd 3: Working in rnds, ch 5, [tr in next tr, ch 1] across, end with ch 1, tr in top of beg ch 4 of row 2, ch 1, join with sl st in 4th ch of beg ch-5, turn. Fasten off.

Rnd 4: Join light green with sl st in first ch-1 sp, ch 4, 4 tr in same ch sp, [ch 2, sk 2 ch sps, 5 tr in next ch sp] around, ch 2, join with sl st in top of beg ch-4. *(210 tr)*

Rnd 5: Ch 4, **tr dec** *(see Special Stitch)* in next 4 sts, [ch 8, tr dec in next 5 sts] around, ending with ch 8, join with sl st in top of beg ch-4. Fasten off. *(42 tr dec)*

Rnd 6: Join yellow with sl st in first tr dec, ch 4, [9 tr in next ch-8 sp, tr in next tr dec) around, ending with 9 tr in last ch-8 sp, join with sl st in top of beg ch-4. Fasten off. *(420 tr)*

Rnd 7: Join dark pink with sl st in 5th tr of tr group, ch 4, 4 tr in same tr, *ch 3, sk next 4 tr, (sc, ch 4, sc) in next tr, ch 3, sk next 4 tr**, 5 tr in next tr, rep from * around, ending last rep at **, join with sl st in top of beg ch-4.

Rnd 8: Ch 4, tr dec in next 4 sts, *ch 5, tr dec in next 2 ch-3 sps, ch 5**, tr dec in next 5 sts, rep from * around, ending last rep at**, join with sl st in top of beg ch-4. Fasten off. *(42 tr dec)*

BARBIE® and associated trademarks are owned by and used with permission from Mattel, Inc. ©2005 Mattel, Inc.

Rnd 9: Join yellow with sl st in any tr dec over ch-3 sps, ch 4, (tr, ch 4, sl st in tr just made for picot, tr) in same st, *ch 5, (sc, ch 4, sc) in next tr dec, ch 5**, (2 tr, picot, tr) in next tr dec, rep from * around, ending last rep at **, join with sl st in top of beg ch-4. Fasten off.

Finishing
Tack 10-inch length of ribbon at center front waist. Sew snaps evenly spaced along back opening.

HAT
Rnd 1: Starting at crown, with yellow, ch 6, sl st in first ch to form ring, ch 3 *(counts as first dc)*, 11 dc in ring, join with sl st in top of beg ch-3. *(12 dc)*

Rnds 2 & 3: Ch 3, dc in same dc, 2 dc in each dc around, join with sl st in top of beg ch-3. *(48 dc at end of rnd 3)*

Rnd 4: Ch 3, working in **back lps** *(see Stitch Guide)* this rnd only, dc in each dc around, join with sl st in top of beg ch-3.

Rnd 5: Ch 1, sc in first dc, [ch 3, sc in next dc] around, ch 3, join with sl st in beg sc. *(48 ch sps)*

Rnd 6: Sl st in first ch sp, ch 1, sc in same ch sp, [ch 3, sc in next ch sp] around, ch 3, join with sl st in top of beg ch-3.

Rnds 7 & 8: Sl st in first ch sp, ch 1, sc in same ch sp, [ch 4, sc in next sp] around, ch 4, join with sl st in beg sc. At end of last rnd, fasten off.

Flowers
Make 4 dark pink.
Make 2 each light green & light blue.
Ch 4, 2 dc in 4th ch from hook, ch 3, sl st in same ch, *(ch 3, 2 dc, ch 3, sl st) in same ch, rep from * twice. Leaving a 6-inch end, fasten off,

Sew Flowers around Hat, alternating colors and leaving 1-inch circle free at crown.

Weave 10-inch length of ribbon in and out across RS of crown on rnd 4. ❑❑

All That Glitters

Designs by Juanita Turner

GOLD GOWN

SKILL LEVEL

INTERMEDIATE

FINISHED SIZE

Fits 11½-inch fashion doll

MATERIALS

❑ Lamé thread:
    95 yds gold
❑ Size 7/1.65mm steel crochet hook or size needed to obtain gauge
❑ Sewing needle
❑ Gold sewing thread
❑ 3 small snaps

GAUGE

9 sc = 1 inch; 9 sc rows = 1 inch

INSTRUCTIONS

GOWN

Skirt

Row 1: Starting at waist, ch 26, sc in 2nd ch from hook and in each ch across, turn. *(25 sc)*

Row 2: Ch 1, sc in each st across, turn.

Row 3: Ch 1, sc in each of first 2 sts, 2 sc in each of next 21 sts, sc in each of last 2 sts, turn. *(46 sc)*

Rows 4–11: Ch 1, sc in each st across, turn.

Rnd 12: Lap last 2 sts of this rnd over first 2 sts, working through both thicknesses, sl st in last st and 2nd st of this rnd, ch 1, sc in same st as sl st, sc in each st around, join with sl st in beg sc, **turn.** *(44 sc)*

Rnd 13: Ch 1, sc in each of first 8 sts, **sc dec** *(see Stitch Guide)* in next 2 sts, sc in each of next 24 sts, sc dec in next 2 sts, sc in each of last 8 sts, join with sl st in beg sc, turn. *(42 sc)*

Rnd 14: Ch 1, sc in each of first 8 sts, sc dec in next 2 sts, sc in each of next 22 sts, sc dec in next 2 sts, sc in each of last 8 sts, join with sl st in beg sc, turn. *(40 sc)*

Rnd 15: Ch 1, sc in each of first 8 sts, sc dec in next 2 sts, sc in each of next 20 sts, sc dec in next 2 sts,

BARBIE® and associated trademarks are owned by and used with permission from Mattel, Inc. ©2005 Mattel, Inc.

sc in each of last 8 sts, join with sl st in beg sc, turn. *(38 sc)*

Rnd 16: Ch 1, sc in each st around, join with sl st in beg sc, turn.

Rnd 17: Ch 1, sc in each of first 8 sts, sc dec in next 2 sts, sc in each of next 18 sts, sc dec in next 2 sts, sc in each of last 8 sts, join with sl st in beg sc, turn. *(36 sc)*

Rnd 18: Ch 1, sc in each of first 8 sts, sc dec in next 2 sts, sc in each of next 16 sts, sc dec in next 2 sts, sc in each of last 8 sts, join with sl st in beg sc, turn. *(34 sc)*

Rnd 19: Ch 1, sc in each of first 8 sts, sc dec in next 2 sts, sc in each of next 14 sts, sc dec in next 2 sts, sc in each of last 8 sts, join with sl st in beg sc, turn. *(32 sc)*

Rnd 20: Ch 1, sc in each st around, join with sl st in beg sc, turn.

Rnd 21: Ch 1, sc in each of first 8

sts, sc dec in next 2 sts, sc in each of next 12 sts, sc dec in next 2 sts, sc in each of last 8 sts, join with sl st in beg sc, turn. (30 sc)

Rnd 22: Ch 1, sc in each st around, join with sl st in beg sc, turn.

Rnd 23: Ch 1, sc in each of first 8 sts, sc dec in next 2 sts, sc in each of next 10 sts, sc dec in next 2 sts, sc in each of last 8 sts, join with sl st in beg sc, turn. (28 sc)

Rnds 24–26: Ch 1, sc in each st around, join with sl st in beg sc, turn. At end of last rnd, fasten off.

Side Slit

Row 27: Count over 9 sts to the right of the joining sl st at center back of Skirt, join with sc in next st, sc in each of skipped 9 sts and in each of next 16 sts, leaving last 2 sts unworked, turn. (26 sc)

Row 28: Ch 1, sc in each st across, turn.

Row 29: Ch 1, sc in each of first 16 sts, 2 sc in each of next 2 sts, sc in each of last 8 sts, turn. (28 sc)

Rows 30–43: Ch 1, sc in each st across, turn.

Row 44: Ch 1, sc in first st, sc dec in next 2 sts, sc in each of next 15 sts, 2 sc in each of next 2 sts, sc in each of last 5 sts, sc dec in next 2 sts, sc in last st, turn.

Rows 45–47: Ch 1, sc in each of first 3 sts, hdc in each of next 22 sts, sc in each of last 3 sts, turn. (28 sts)

Row 48: Ch 1, sc in first st, sc dec in next 2 sts, sc in each of next 22 sts, sc dec in next 2 sts, sc in last st, turn. (26 sc)

Row 49: Ch 1, sk first st, sc in next st, hdc in each of next 22 sts, sc in next st, sk last st, sl st in end of row 48, **do not turn.**

Rnd 50: Ch 1, sc in end of each row down 1 side of slit, sc dec in next 2 unworked sts of row 26, sc in end of each row down 2nd side of slit, sc in each st across row 49, join with sl st in beg sc. Fasten off.

Bodice

Row 1: Working in starting ch on opposite side of row 1 of Skirt, join with sc in first ch, sc in each of next 4 chs, sc dec in next 2 chs, sc in each of next 11 chs, sc dec in next 2 chs, sc

in each of last 5 sts, turn. (23 sc)

Rows 2–5: Ch 1, sc in each st across, turn.

Row 6: Ch 1, sc in first st, sc dec in next 2 sts, sc in each of next 17 sts, sc dec in next 2 sts, sc in last st, turn. (21 sc)

Row 7: Ch 1, sc in each st across, turn.

Row 8: Ch 1, sc in first st, sc dec in next 2 sts, sc in each of next 15 sts, sc dec in next 2 sts, sc in last st, turn. (19 sc)

Rows 9 & 10: Ch 1, sc in each st across, turn.

Row 11: Ch 1, sc in first st, sc dec in next 2 sts, sc in next st, [sk next st, 3 dc in each of next 3 sts, sk next st, sc in next st] twice, sc dec in next 2 sts, sc in last st, turn. (25 sts)

Row 12: Ch 1, sc in each of first 2 sts, sk next st, dc in each of next 8 sts, sk next st, sc in next st, sk next st, dc in each of next 8 sts, sk next st, sc in each of last 2 sts, turn. (21 sts)

Row 13: Ch 1, sk first st, sl st in next st, sc in each of next 17 sts, sk next st, sl st in last st. Fasten off.

Collar

Row 1: Ch 18, sc in 2nd ch from hook, sc in each of next 7 chs, (sc, ch 1, sc) in next ch, sc in each of last 8 chs, turn. (18 sc)

Row 2: Ch 1, 2 sc in first st, sc in each of next 6 sts, work steps A–E to finish Collar on Bodice:

A. Holding back of Bodice facing you, dtr in sl st on right side of last row on Bodice, sc in next st on row 1 of Collar;

B. Sk next 2 sts on Bodice, dtr in next st, sc in next st on Collar, sk next 2 sts on Bodice, dtr in next st on Bodice;

C. (Sc, ch 3, sc) in ch-1 sp on Collar, sc in next st on Bodice, sk next 5 sts on Bodice, dtr in next st on Bodice;

D. Sc in next st on row 1 of Collar, sk next 2 sts on Bodice, dtr in next st, sc in next st on Collar;

E. Sk next 2 sts on Bodice, dtr in last sl st on Bodice, sc in each of last 6 sts on Collar. Fasten off.

Sew 1 snap to back of Collar, 1 to waist and 1 halfway below waist at back of Gown.

MULTICOLORED GOWN

SKILL LEVEL

INTERMEDIATE

FINISHED SIZE

Fits 11½-inch fashion doll

MATERIALS

- ❏ Crochet cotton size 10:
    95 yds black
- ❏ 95 yds multicolored blending filament
- ❏ Size 7/1.65mm steel crochet hook or size needed to obtain gauge
- ❏ Sewing needle
- ❏ Black sewing thread
- ❏ 1 small snap

GAUGE

9 sc = 1 inch; 9 sc rows = 1 inch

PATTERN NOTE

Work with 1 strand each black crochet cotton and multicolored blending filament held together as 1 throughout.

SPECIAL STITCH

Long single crochet (long sc): *(See illustration),* insert hook between dc, complete as sc.

Long Single Crochet

INSTRUCTIONS

GOWN

Skirt

Row 1: Starting at waist, ch 26, sc in 2nd ch from hook and in each ch across, turn. (25 sc)

Row 2: Ch 1, sc in each st across, turn.

Row 3: Ch 1, sc in each of first 2 sts, 2 sc in each of next 21 sts, sc in each of last 2 sts, turn. (46 sc)

Rows 4–11: Ch 1, sc in each st across, turn.

Rnd 12: Lap last 2 sts of this rnd over first 2 sts. Working through both thicknesses, sl st in last st and 2nd st of this rnd, ch 1, sc in same st as sl st, sc in each st around, join with sl st in first sc, **turn.** (44 sc)

Rnd 13: Ch 1, sc in each of first 8 sts, **sc dec** (see Stitch Guide) in next 2 sts, sc in each of next 24 sts, sc dec in next 2 sts, sc in each of last 8 sts, join with sl st in beg sc, turn. (42 sc)

Rnd 14: Ch 1, sc in each of first 8 sts, sc dec in next 2 sts, sc in each of next 22 sts, sc dec in next 2 sts, sc in each of last 8 sts, join with sl st in beg sc, turn. (40 sc)

Rnds 15–20: Ch 1, sc in each st across, join with sl st in beg sc, turn.

Rnd 21: Ch 1, sc in each of first 8 sts, sc dec in next 2 sts, sc in each of next 20 sts, sc dec in next 2 sts, sc in each of last 8 sts, join with sl st in beg sc, turn. (38 sc)

Rnds 22–25: Ch 1, sc in each st across, join with sl st in beg sc, turn.

Back Slit

Row 26: Working in rows, ch 1, sc in each st across, turn.

Row 27: Ch 1, sc in each of first 8 sts, sc dec in next 2 sts, sc in each of next 18 sts, sc dec in next 2 sts, sc in each of last 8 sts, turn. (36 sc)

Rows 28–33: Ch 1, sc in each st across, turn.

Rows 34: Ch 1, sc in each of first 8 sts, sc dec in next 2 sts, sc in each of next 16 sts, sc dec in next 2 sts, sc in each of last 8 sts, turn. (34 sc)

Rows 35–38: Ch 1, sc in each st across, turn.

Row 39: Ch 1, sc in each of first 8 sts, sc dec in next 2 sts, sc in each of next 14 sts, sc dec in next 2 sts, sc in each of last 8 sts, turn. (32 sc)

Rows 40–51: Ch 1, sc in each st across, turn.

Row 52: Ch 1, sc in each of first 3 sts, 2 sc in next st, [sc in each of next 3 sts, 2 sc in next st] across, turn. (40 sc)

Rows 53–58: Ch 1, sc in each st across, turn. At end of row last row, **do not turn.**

Rnd 59: Working in sts and ends of rows, ch 1, 2 sc in end of first row, work steps A–E to finish rnd:

A. Sc in end of each row across first side of slit with sl st in end of row 26;

B. Working on 2nd side of slit, sl st in end of row 26, sc in each row across with 2 sc in last row;

C. Working across row 58, (sl st, ch 3, 2 dc) in first st, sk next st;

D. (Sl st, ch 3, 2 dc) in next st, sk next st;

E. Rep step D across, join with sl st in beg sc. Fasten off.

Bodice

Row 1: Working in starting ch on opposite side of row 1 on Skirt, join with sc in first ch, sc in each of next 4 chs, sc dec in next 2 chs, sc in each of next 11 chs, sc dec in next 2 chs, sc in each of last 5 sts, turn. (23 sc)

Rows 2–5: Ch 1, sc in each st across, turn.

Row 6: Ch 1, sc in first st, sc dec in next 2 sts, sc in each of next 17 sts, sc dec in next 2 sts, sc in last st, turn. (21 sc)

Rows 7–10: Ch 1, sc in each st across, turn.

Row 11: Ch 1, sc in each of first 5 sts, sk next st, 3 dc in each of next 3 sts, sk next st, sc in next st, sk next st, 3 dc in each of next 3 sts, sk next st, sc in each of last 5 sts, turn. (29 sts)

Row 12: Ch 1, sc in each of first 4 sts, sk next st, dc in each of next 8 sts, sk next st, sc in next st, sk next st, dc in each of next 8 sts, sk next st, sc in each of last 4 sts, turn. (25 sts)

Row 13: Ch 1, sc in first st, sc dec in next 2 sts, sk next st, sc in next 17 sts, sk next st, sc dec in next 2 sts, sc in last st, turn.

Row 14: Ch 1, sc in first st, sk next st, sc in each of next 8 sts, inserting hook in top of sc between 2 dc work a **long sc** (see Special Stitches), sc in each of next 8 sts, sk next st, sc in last st, turn, **do not fasten off.**

First Strap

Sl st in first st, ch 6, sk next 2 sts on Bodice, work steps A–F to complete Strap:

A. Yo 4 times, insert hook in next st, yo, pull through st, (yo, pull through 2 lps on hook) 4 times;

B. Yo 4 times, insert hook in next st, yo, pull through st, (yo, pull through 2 lps on hook) 4 times, yo, pull through all lps on hook;

C. Ch 18, sl st in end of row 10 on opposite side of Bodice back;

D. Sl st in end of each row down to row 6;

E. Ch 17, sk first 2 chs of ch 18, sl st in next ch;

F. Ch 18, sl st in end of row 2, sl st in end of row 1. Fasten off.

Second Strap

Join with sl st in first st on unworked end of row 14 on Bodice, ch 6, sk next 2 sts on Bodice, work steps A–F to finish Strap overlapping the Straps:

A. Yo 4 times, insert hook in next st, yo, pull through st, [yo, pull through 2 lps on hook] 4 times;

B. Yo 4 times, insert hook in next st, yo, pull through st, [yo, pull through 2 lps on hook] 4 times, yo, pull through all lps on hook;

C. Ch 18, sl st in end of row 10 on opposite side of Bodice back;

D. Sl st in end of each row down to row 6;

E. Ch 17, sk first 2 chs of ch 18, sl st in next ch;

F. Ch 18, sl st in end of row 2, sl st in end of row 1. Fasten off.

SNOOD

Rnd 1: Ch 6, sl st in first ch to form ring, ch 6, [dc in ring, ch 3] 4 times, (dc, ch 2) in ring, join with dc in 3rd ch of ch 6 forming last ch sp. (6 ch sps)

Rnd 2: Sl st in ch sp just made, ch 8 (counts as first dc and ch 5), [dc in next ch sp, ch 5] 4 times, dc in next ch sp, ch 3, join with dc in 3rd ch of beg ch-8 forming last ch sp.

Rnd 3: Ch 1, sc in ch sp just made, *(ch 5, sc) twice in next ch sp**, ch 5, sc in next ch sp, rep from * around, ending last rep at **, ch 3, join with dc in first sc forming last ch sp. (9 ch sps)

Rnds 4–7: Ch 1, sc in ch sp just made, [ch 5, sc in next ch sp] around, ch 3, join with dc in beg sc forming last ch sp. At end of last rnd, fasten off.

Drawstring

Ch 100. Fasten off. Weave through ch sps of rnd 7.

Place Snood over bun made on top of doll's head, pulling gently, draw Snood to cup around hair, wind remainder of drawstring around base of Bun.

FINISHING

With black sewing thread and needle, sew 1 snap to back of Gown.

Optional: For earrings and Snood trim, straight pins stuck through seed beads and sequins and into the head of the doll may be evenly spaced around the Snood. ❑❑

Old-Fashioned Living Room

Designs by Mickie Akins

SOFA & CHAIR

SKILL LEVEL

EXPERIENCED

FINISHED SIZES

Sofa: 9½ inches long
Chair: 5 inches long

MATERIALS

- ❏ Fine (sport) weight chenille yarn: 475 yds ruby
- ❏ Size E/4/3.5mm crochet hook or size needed to obtain gauge
- ❏ Tapestry needle
- ❏ Sewing needle
- ❏ Red sewing thread
- ❏ 2 sheets red 7-count plastic canvas
- ❏ Polyester fiberfill
- ❏ 2 dark red 8 x 12-inch pieces felt

GAUGE

5 sts = 1 inch; 4 rows in st pattern = 1 inch

INSTRUCTIONS

SOFA

Back

Row 1: Starting at bottom, ch 85, sc in 2nd ch from hook and in each ch across, turn. *(84 sc)*

Row 2: Ch 1, sc in first sc, dc in next sc, [sc in next sc, dc in next sc] across, turn.

Rows 3–7: Ch 1, sc in first dc, dc in next sc, [sc in next dc, dc in next sc] across, turn.

Row 8: Sl st in each of first 4 sts, ch 1, [sc in next dc, dc in next sc] across to last 4 sts, sk last 4 sts, turn. *(76 sc and dc)*

Row 9: Ch 1, sc in first dc, dc in next sc, [sc in next dc, dc in next sc] across leaving sl sts unworked, turn.

Rows 10–16: Ch 1, sc in first dc, dc in next sc, [sc in next dc, dc in next sc] across, turn.

Row 17: Sl st in each of first 5 sts, ch 1, sk next sc, [sc in next dc, dc in next sc] across to last 6 sts, sk last 6 sts, turn. *(64 sc and dc)*

Row 18: Sl st in first dc, ch 1, sk next sc, [sc in next dc, dc in next sc] across, turn. *(62 sc and dc)*

Row 19: Sl st in first dc, ch 1, sk next sc, [sc in next dc, dc in next sc] across, turn. *(60 sc and dc)*

Row 20: Sl st in first dc, ch 1, sk next sc, [sc in next dc, dc in next sc] across to last 2 sts, sl st in next dc, sk last sc, turn. *(56 sc and dc)*

Row 21: Ch 1, sk sl st, sl st in next dc, ch 1, sk next sc, [sc in next dc, dc in next sc] across to last 2 sts, sl st in next dc, sk last sc, turn. *(52 sc and dc)*

Row 22: Sl st in each st across. Fasten off.

Using crochet piece as pattern, cut piece from plastic canvas. Label plastic canvas piece for future reference.

Bottom Front

Row 1: Ch 47, sc in 2nd ch from hook and in each ch across, turn. *(46 sc)*

Row 2: Ch 1, sc in first sc, dc in next sc, [sc in next sc, dc in next sc] across, turn.

Rows 3–6: Ch 1, sc in first dc, dc in next sc, [sc in next dc, dc in next sc] across, turn.

Row 7: Ch 1, sc in each st across, turn.

Using crochet piece as pattern, cut 2 pieces from plastic canvas for Bottom Front and Back, then label.

Seat

Row 8: Working this row in **front lps** *(see Stitch Guide)*, ch 1, sc in each st across, turn.

BARBIE® and associated trademarks are owned by and used with permission from Mattel, Inc. ©2005 Mattel, Inc.

Row 9: Ch 1, sc in first sc, dc in next sc, [sc in next sc, dc in next sc] across, turn.

Rows 10–11: Ch 1, sc in first dc, dc in next sc, [sc in next dc, dc in next sc] across, turn.

Row 12: Sl st in each of first 4 sts, ch 1, [sc in next dc, dc in next sc] across to last 4 sts, sk last 4 sts, turn. *(38 sc and dc)*

Row 13: Ch 1, sc in first dc, dc in next sc, (sc in next dc, dc in next sc) across leaving sl sts unworked, turn.

Rows 14–20: Ch 1, sc in first dc, dc in next sc, [sc in next dc, sc in next sc] across, turn.

Row 21: Sl st in first dc, ch 1, sk next sc, [sc in next dc, dc in next sc] across to last 2 sts, sk next dc, sl st in last sc. Fasten off.

Using rows 8–21 as pattern, cut piece from plastic canvas and label.

Top Front & Arm Ends

Row 1: Ch 67, sc in 2nd ch from hook and in each ch across, turn. *(66 sc)*

Row 2: Ch 1, sc in first sc, dc in next sc, [sc in next sc, dc in next sc] across, turn.

Rows 3–10: Ch 1, sc in first dc, dc in next sc, [sc in next dc, dc in next sc] across, turn.

Row 11: For **top edges**, sl st in each of first 14 sts, ch 1, [sc in next dc, dc in next sc] across to last 14 sts, sk last 14 sts, turn. *(38 sc and dc)*

Row 12: Sl st in first dc, ch 1, sk next sc, [sc in next dc, dc in next sc] across to last 2 sts, sl st in next dc, sk last sc and sl sts, turn. *(34 sc and dc)*

Row 13: Sl st in first dc, ch 1, sk next sc, [sc in next dc, dc in next sc] across to last 2 sts, sk next dc, sl st in last sc. Fasten off.

Top Strip

Row 1: Ch 70, hdc in 3rd ch from hook, hdc in each of next 10 chs, 2 hdc in next ch, hdc in next ch, 2 hdc in next ch, hdc in each of next 39 chs, 2 hdc in next ch, hdc in next ch, 2 hdc in next ch, hdc in each of last 12 chs, turn. *(73 hdc)*

Row 2: Ch 2, hdc in each st across. Fasten off.

Cushion

Row 1: Starting at back, ch 31, sc in 2nd ch from hook and in each ch across, turn. *(30 sc)*

Row 2: Ch 1, (sc, dc) in each of first 2 sc, [sc in next sc, dc in next sc] across to last 2 sc, (sc, dc) in each of last 2 sc, turn. *(34 sc and dc)*

Row 3: Ch 1, sc in first dc, dc in next sc, [sc in next dc, dc in next sc] across, turn.

Row 4: Ch 1, (sc, dc) in each of first 2 sts, [sc in next dc, dc in next sc] across to last 2 sts, (sc, dc) in each of last 2 sts, turn. *(38 sc and dc)*

Rows 5–9: Ch 1, sc in first dc, dc in next sc, [sc in next dc, dc in next sc] across, turn. At end of last row, fasten off.

Row 10: Ch 4, join with sc in first dc, dc in next sc, [sc in next dc, dc in next sc] across, ch 5, turn.

Row 11: Sc in 2nd ch from hook, dc in next ch, sc in next ch, dc in next ch, [sc in next dc, dc in next sc] across to last dc, sc in last dc, dc in last sc, [sc in next ch, dc in next ch] twice, turn. *(46 sc and dc)*

Rows 12–19: Ch 1, sc in first dc, dc in next sc, [sc in next dc, dc in next sc] across, turn.

Row 20: Sl st in each of first 4 sts, ch 1, sc in next dc, dc in next sc, [sc in next dc, dc in next sc] across to last 4 sts, sk last 4 sts, turn. *(38 sc and dc)*

Rows 21–25: Ch 1, sc in first dc, dc in next sc, [sc in next dc, dc in next sc] across, turn.

Rows 26 & 27: Ch 1, **sc dec** *(see Stitch Guide)* in first 2 sts, **dc dec** *(see Stitch Guide)* in next 2 sts, [sc in next dc, dc in next sc] across to last 4 sts, sc dec in next 2 sts, dc dec in last 2 sts, turn. Fasten off. *(30 sc and dc at end of row 27)*

Cushion Strip

Row 1: Ch 76, sc in 2nd ch from hook and in each ch across, turn. *(75 sc)*

Row 2: Ch 1, sc in first st, dc in next st, [sc in next st, dc in next st] across, turn.

Row 3: Ch 1, sc in each st across. Fasten off.

Fold Cushion in half, with tapestry needle and yarn, matching ends of Cushion Strip to ends of rows 13–15 on each side of Cushion, sew Cushion Strip to outer edges of Cushion, stuffing before closing.

Frame Assembly

1. For **Arm Ends,** cut 2 pieces from plastic canvas each 4 x 12 holes.

2. Whipstitch plastic canvas Bottom Front and Bottom Back to Seat *(see Illustration 1).*

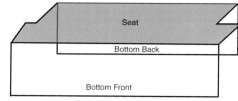

Illustration 1

2. Wrap plastic canvas Back around assembled Bottom, whipstitch ends of pieces tog *(see dotted line on Illustration 2).*

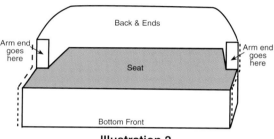

Illustration 2

3. Whipstitch Arm Ends to assembled pieces according to Illustration 2.

4. For **Bottom,** using bottom edges of assembled Frame as pattern, cut 1 piece from plastic canvas and 1 piece from felt.

Sofa Cover Assembly

1. Sew Top Strip to Top Front, matching ends of rows on Strip to unworked sts at ends of row 11 and Front, and easing starting ch on Strip to fit remainder of top edge on Front *(see dotted line on Illustration 3).*

Top Front goes here

Illustration 3

2. Sew row 1 on Top Front to back of Seat across rows 12–21 *(see dotted line on Illustration 4).*

Seat

Illustration 4

3. Leaving bottom edges open, sew rem edges of Cover Back to Bottom Front, Seat, Top Front and Top Strip.
4. Place assembled Cover over Frame, stuff between plastic canvas and Top Front. Tack inside seam of Top Front and Seat to back edge of plastic canvas Seat. Stuff inside of Seat.
5. Whipstitch plastic canvas Bottom to bottom edges of plastic canvas Frame. Sew felt Bottom to bottom edges of assembled Cover.
6. Place Cushion on Seat.

CHAIR
Back
With ch 61, work same as Sofa Back.

Bottom Front & Seat
With ch 25, work same as Sofa Bottom Front & Seat.

Top Front & Arm Ends
With ch 45, work same as Sofa Top Front & Arm Ends.

Top Strip
Row 1: Ch 48, hdc in 3rd ch from hook *(first 2 chs count as first hdc)*, hdc in each of next 9 chs, [2 hdc in next ch, hdc in next ch] twice, hdc in each of next 18 chs, [2 hdc in next ch, hdc in next ch] twice, hdc in each of last 10 chs, turn. *(51 sc)*
Row 2: Ch 2, hdc in each st across. Fasten off.

Cushion
Row 1: Starting at back, ch 9, sc in 2nd ch from hook and in each ch across, turn. *(8 sc)*
Row 2: Ch 1, (sc, dc) in each of first 2 sc, [sc in next sc, dc in next sc] across to last 2 sc, (sc, dc) in each of last 2 sc, turn. *(12 sc and dc)*
Row 3: Ch 1, sc in first dc, dc in next sc, [sc in next dc, dc in next sc] across, turn.
Row 4: Ch 1, (sc, dc) in each of first 2 sts, [sc in next dc, dc in next sc] across to last 2 sts, (sc, dc) in each of last 2 sts, turn. *(16 sc and dc)*
Rows 5–9: Ch 1, sc in first dc, dc in next sc, [sc in next dc, dc in next sc] across, turn. At end of last row, fasten off.
Row 10: Ch 4, join with sc in first dc, dc in next sc, [sc in next dc, dc in next sc]

across, ch 5, turn.
Row 11: Sc in 2nd ch from hook, dc in next ch, sc in next ch, dc in next ch, [sc in next dc, dc in next sc] across to last dc, sc in last dc, dc in last sc, [sc in next ch, dc in next ch] twice, turn. *(24 sc and dc)*
Rows 12–19: Ch 1, sc in first dc, dc in next sc, [sc in next dc, dc in next sc] across, turn.
Row 20: Sl st in each of first 4 sts, ch 1, [sc in next dc, dc in next sc] across to last 4 sts, sk last 4 sts, turn. *(16 sc and dc)*
Rows 21–25: Ch 1, sc in first dc, dc in next sc, [sc in next dc, dc in next sc] across, turn.
Rows 26 & 27: Ch 1, sc dec in first 2 sts, dc dec in next 2 sts, [sc in next dc, dc in next sc] across to last 4 sts, sc dec in next 2 sts, dc dec in last 2 sts, turn. At end of last row, fasten off. *(12 sc and dc, 8 sc and dc)*

Cushion Strip
Row 1: Ch 51, sc in 2nd ch from hook and in each ch across, turn. *(50 sc)*
Row 2: Ch 1, sc in first st, dc in next st, [sc in next st, dc in next st] across, turn.
Row 3: Ch 1, sc in each st across. At end of last row, fasten off.
Fold Cushion in half, matching ends of Cushion Strip to ends of rows 13–15 on each side of Cushion, sew Cushion Strip to outer edges of Cushion, stuffing before closing.

Frame Assembly
Work same as Sofa Frame Assembly.

Cover Assembly
Work same as Sofa Cover Assembly.

COFFEE & END TABLES
SKILL LEVEL
◼◼◼▢

INTERMEDIATE

FINISHED SIZES
Coffee Table: 3¼ x 6¼ x 2¼ inches tall
End Table: 2¾ inches square x 2¾ inches tall

MATERIALS
❏ Pearl crochet cotton size 3:
   120 yds black

❏ Size 7/1.65mm steel crochet hook or size needed to obtain gauge
❏ Large-eye embroidery needle
❏ ¼-inch dowel:
   4 pieces, each 2 inches long
   4 pieces, each 2½ inches long
❏ 3 x 6-inch piece of 1/16-inch-thick styrene sheet
❏ 1 sheet black 7-count plastic canvas
❏ Glue gun and glue

GAUGE
7 sts = 1 inch; 1 dc row = ¼ inch; 5 hdc rows = 1 inch

INSTRUCTIONS
COFFEE TABLE
Leg Cover
Make 4.
Row 1: Ch 17, sc in 2nd ch from hook and in each ch across, turn. *(16 sc)*
Rows 2–9: Working in **back lps** *(see Stitch Guide)*, ch 1, sc in each st across, turn. At end of last row, leave 8-inch end for sewing. Fasten off.

Leg Assembly
Wrap Leg Cover over 1 (2-inch) dowel, matching sts, sew row 1 to row 9. Sew openings closed at each end. Repeat for each 2-inch dowel.

Frame
1. For **Sides**, cut 2 pieces, each 3 x 39 holes, from plastic canvas.
2. For **Ends**, cut 2 pieces, each 3 x 18-hole from plastic canvas.
3. For **Top**, cut a 19 x 39-hole piece from plastic canvas, cut center out leaving a 2-hole-wide strip around all edges.
4. Whipstitch short edges on Ends and Sides tog, matching edges, whipstitch Top to long edges on Ends and Sides.
5. Glue styrene sheet to top of Frame Top.

Top Cover
Rnd 1: Ch 102 *(check to make sure it fits around Table Sides and Ends)*, being careful not to twist ch, sl st in first ch to form ring, ch 3 *(counts as first dc)*, 2 dc in same ch, *dc in each of next 36 chs, 3 dc in next ch, dc in each of next 13 chs*, 3 dc in next

ch, rep between *, join with sl st in 3rd ch of beg ch-3. Center st of 3-dc group is corner st. *(110 dc)*

Rnd 2: Ch 2 *(counts as first hdc)*, 3 hdc in next st, hdc in each st across to next corner st, [3 hdc in corner st, hdc in each st across to next corner st] around, join with sl st in 2nd ch of beg ch-2. *(118 hdc)*

Rnd 3: Ch 1, sc in each of first 2 sts, *3 sc in next st, sc in each of next 40 sts, 3 sc in next st*, sc in each of next 17 sts, rep between *, sc in each st around, join with sl st in beg sc. *(126 sc)*

Rnd 4: Working this rnd in back lps, ch 3, dc in each st around, join with sl st in 3rd ch of beg ch-3.

Rnd 5: Ch 3, dc in next st, *dc dec *(see Stitch Guide)* in next 3 sts, dc in each of next 40 sts, dc dec in next 3 sts*, dc in each of next 17 sts, rep between *, dc in each st around, join with sl st in 3rd ch of beg ch-3. Fasten off.

Glue WS of Top Cover to Front Sides, Ends and styrene.

Glue 1 end of each Leg to inside corners of Top.

END TABLE
Leg Cover
Make 4.

With ch 20, work same as Coffee Table Leg.

Leg Assembly

With 2½-inch dowels, work same as Coffee Table Leg Assembly.

Frame

1. For **Sides,** cut 2 pieces, each 3 x 16-hole pieces from plastic canvas.

2. For **Top,** cut a 16 x 16-hole piece from plastic canvas.

3. Whipstitch short edges on Sides tog, whipstitch Top to long edges on Sides.

Top Cover

Rnd 1: Ch 2, 8 sc in 2nd ch from hook, join with sl st in beg sc. *(8 sc)*

Rnd 2: Ch 2, 3 hdc in next st, [hdc in next st, 3 hdc in next st] around, join with sl st in 3rd ch of beg ch-2. *(16 hdc)*

Rnd 3: Ch 2, hdc in next st, 5 hdc in next st, [hdc in next 3 sts, 5

hdc in next st] 3 times, hdc in last st, join with sl st in 2nd ch of beg ch-2. *(32 hdc)*

Rnds 4 & 5: Ch 2, [hdc in each st across to center st of next corner group, 5 hdc in center st] 4 times, hdc in each st across, join with sl st in 2nd ch of beg ch-2. *(64 hdc at end of rnd 5)*

Rnds 6 & 7: Ch 2, [hdc in each st across to center st of next corner group, 3 hdc in center st] 4 times, hdc in each st across, join with sl st in 2nd ch of beg ch-2. *(80 hdc at end of rnd 7)*

Rnd 8: Working this rnd in back lps, ch 2, hdc in each st around, join with sl st in 2nd ch of beg ch-2.

Rnds 9 & 10: Ch 2, hdc in each st around, join with sl st in 2nd ch of beg ch-2. At end of last rnd, fasten off.

Glue WS of Top Cover to Top and Sides.

Glue 1 end of each Leg to inside corners of Top.

PILLOWS
SKILL LEVEL

EASY

FINISHED SIZES

Round pillow: 2½ inches across
Square Pillow: 2½ inches square

MATERIALS

❑ Fine (sport) weight chenille yarn: 50 yds white
❑ Crochet cotton size 10: 40 yds white
❑ Fine (sport) weight woven acrylic yarn: 10 yds cream
❑ Size 7/1.65mm steel crochet hook or size needed to obtain gauge
❑ Size C/2/2.75mm crochet hook or size needed to obtain gauge
❑ Tapestry needle
❑ Large-eye embroidery needle
❑ Polyester fiberfill

GAUGE

Size 7 hook and thread: 8 sts = 1 inch; 6 hdc rows = 1 inch
Size C hook and chenille yarn: Rnds 1 and 2 = 1¼ inches across

SPECIAL STITCH

Cluster (cl): Yo, insert hook in next ch sp, yo, pull through ch sp, yo, pull through 2 lps on hook, [yo, insert hook in same ch sp, yo, pull through ch sp, yo, pull through 2 lps on hook] twice, yo, pull through all lps on hook.

INSTRUCTIONS
ROUND PILLOW
Side
Make 2.

Rnd 1: With white chenille yarn and size C hook, ch 4, 11 dc in 4th ch from hook, join with sl st in 4th ch of beg ch-4. *(12 dc)*

Rnd 2: Ch 3 *(counts as first dc)*, dc in same st, 2 dc in each st around, join with sl st in 3rd ch of beg ch-3. *(24 dc)*

Rnd 3: Working this rnd in **back lps** *(see Stitch Guide)*, ch 1, sc in each st around, **do not join**, mark first st of each rnd.

Rnd 4: Working this rnd in back lps, ch 1, sc in each of first 3 sts, 2 sc in next st, [sc in each of next 3 sts, 2 sc in next st] around, **do not join.** *(30 sc)*

Rnd 5: Working this rnd in back lps, sc in each of first 4 sts, 2 sc in next st, [sc in each of next 4 sts, 2 sc in next st] around, join with sl st in beg sc. For **first Side,** fasten off, for **2nd Side,** do not fasten off.

Rnd 6: Hold Sides WS tog, working through both thicknesses, ch 1, sc in first st, ch 1, [sc in next st, ch 1] around, stuffing before closing, join with sl st in beg sc. Fasten off.

SQUARE PILLOW
Side
Make 2.

Row 1: With white crochet cotton and size 7 hook, ch 21, hdc in 3rd ch from hook and in each ch across, turn. *(20 hdc)*

Rows 2–13: Ch 2, hdc in each st across, turn. At end of last row, fasten off.

Cover

Rnd 1: With acrylic yarn and size 7 hook, ch 4, sl st in first ch to form ring, ch 3, 2 dc in ring, [ch 1, 5 dc in ring] 3 times, ch 1, 2 dc in ring, join with sl st in 3rd ch of beg ch-3. *(20 dc, 4 ch-1 sps)*

Rnd 2: Ch 3, dc in same st, dc in next

st, **cl** (see Special Stitch), ch 2, cl in same ch sp as last cl made, *sk next st, dc in next st, 2 dc in next st, dc in next st, sk next st, (cl, ch 2, cl) in next ch-1 sp, rep from * twice, sk next st, dc in last st, join with sl st in 3rd ch of beg ch-3.

Rnd 3: Ch 1, sc in first st, ch 5, (cl, ch 2, cl) in next ch sp, *ch 5, sk next 2 sts, sc in next st, ch 5, (cl, ch 2, cl) in next ch sp, rep from * twice, ch 5, sk last st, join with sl st in beg sc.

Rnd 4: Ch 1, sc in first st, 5 sc in next ch sp, *(cl, ch 3, cl) in next ch sp, 5 sc in next ch sp**, sc in next sc, 5 sc in next ch sp, rep from * around, ending last rep at **, join with sl st in beg sc. Fasten off.

Center and tack Cover on 1 Side for front.

Rnd 5: Hold WS tog with front facing, working through both thicknesses around outer edge of Sides, join acrylic yarn with sc in any corner st, ch 1, [sc in next st or end of next row, ch 1] around, stuffing before closing, join with sl st in beg sc. Fasten off.

DOILY

SKILL LEVEL

EASY

FINISHED SIZE
2¼ inches across

MATERIALS
- ❑ Crochet cotton size 20:
  30 yds white
- ❑ Size 10/1.15mm steel crochet hook

INSTRUCTIONS
DOILY
Rnd 1: Ch 4, sl st in first ch to form ring, ch 3 (counts as first dc), 17 dc in ring, join with sl st in 3rd ch of beg ch-3. (18 dc)

Rnd 2: Ch 4 (counts as first dc and ch 1), [dc in next st, ch 1] around, join with sl st in 3rd ch of beg ch-4.

Rnd 3: Sl st in first ch sp, ch 5 (counts as first dc and ch 2), [dc in next ch sp, ch 2] around, join with sl st in 3rd ch of beg ch-5.

Rnd 4: Sl st in first ch sp, ch 6 (counts as first dc and ch 3), [dc in next ch sp, ch 3] around, join with sl st in 3rd ch of beg ch-6.

Rnd 5: Ch 1, (sc, hdc, dc, tr, dc, hdc, sc) in each ch sp around, join with sl st in beg sc. Fasten off.

ANTIMACASSAR SETS
SKILL LEVEL

INTERMEDIATE

FINISHED SIZES
Sofa Back Cover: 2½ x 4½ inches
Chair Back Cover: 2½ inches square
Arm Covers: 1¾ inches square

MATERIALS
- ❑ Crochet cotton size 20:
  215 yds white
- ❑ Size 10/1.15mm steel crochet hook or size needed to obtain gauge

GAUGE
11 dc = 1 inch; 6 dc rows = 1 inch

SPECIAL STITCHES
Beginning block (beg block): Ch 3 (counts as first dc), dc in each of next 2 sts.

Block: Dc in each of next 2 sts **or** dc in next ch sp, dc in next st.

Mesh: Ch 1, sk next st or ch, dc in next st.

INSTRUCTIONS
CHAIR BACK COVER
Row 1: Ch 33, dc in 4th ch from hook (first 3 chs count as first dc) and in each ch across, turn. (31 dc)

Note: See Special Stitches for beg block, block and mesh to work the following rows.

Rows 2–15: Work according to Chair Cover Graph, turn. At end of last row, fasten off.

SOFA BACK COVER
Row 1: Ch 57, dc in 4th ch from hook and in each ch across, turn. (55 dc)

Note: See Special Stitches for beg block, block and mesh to work the following rows.

Rows 2–15: Work according to Sofa Cover Graph, turn. At end of last row, fasten off.

ARM COVER
Make 4.

Row 1: Ch 23, dc in 4th ch from hook and in each ch across, turn. (21 dc)

Note: See Special Stitches for beg block, block and mesh to work the following rows.

Rows 2–10: Work according to Arm Cover graph, turn. At end of last row, fasten off.

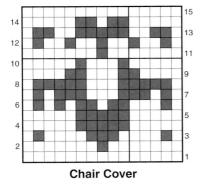
Chair Cover

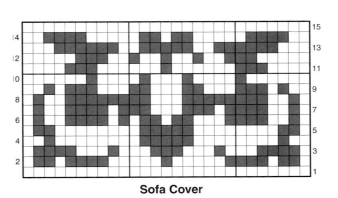
Sofa Cover

STITCH KEY
■ Beg block or block
□ Mesh

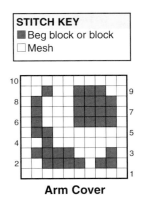
Arm Cover

LAMP

SKILL LEVEL

■■■▭

INTERMEDIATE

FINISHED SIZE

3½ inches tall

MATERIALS

- ❑ Crochet cotton size 20:
  25 yds white
- ❑ Size 10/1.15mm steel hook or size needed to obtain gauge
- ❑ Embroidery needle
- ❑ 3-inch plastic canvas circle
- ❑ 1½-inch-tall wooden spindle
- ❑ Medium wooden candle cup
- ❑ Gold spray paint
- ❑ Fabric stiffener
- ❑ Plastic wrap
- ❑ Glue gun and glue

GAUGE

13 sts = 1½ inches; 7 sc back lp rows = 1 inch

INSTRUCTIONS

LAMP SHADE

Row 1: Ch 14, sc in 2nd ch from hook and in each ch across, turn. *(13 sc)*

Rows 2–33: Working in **back lps** *(see Stitch Guide)*, ch 1, sc in each st across, turn. At end of last row, fasten off. Sew first and last rows tog.

FINISHING

1. For **frame**, cut center 3 rings from plastic canvas circle, discard rem outer piece, cut center bars out of center ring.

2. Stiffen Lamp Shade with fabric stiffener according to manufacturer's instructions.

3. Stuff inside of Lamp Shade with plastic wrap, shaping to fit Frame as it dries, as shown in photo.

4. Insert plastic canvas frame inside Cover and glue in place.

5. Glue spindle and candle cup tog. Paint with gold paint. Let dry.

6. Glue top of spindle to center of frame. ❑❑

Fashion Purses

Designs by Mary Jo Cook

FINISHED SIZE
Accessories for 11½-inch fashion doll

MATERIALS
- ❏ Crochet cotton size 10: assorted colors
- ❏ Size 6/1.80mm steel crochet hook or size needed to obtain gauge

GAUGE
7 dc = 1 inch; 4 dc rows = 1 inch

SPECIAL STITCH
Popcorn (pc): 5 dc in next st, drop lp from hook, insert hook in top of first dc in 5-dc group, pull dropped lp through, ch 1 to secure.

INSTRUCTIONS
ROUND PURSE
Use 1 color
Side
Make 2.

Rnd 1: Ch 5, sl st in first ch to form ring, ch 3 *(counts as first dc)*, 13 dc in ring, join with sl st in 3rd ch of beg ch-3. *(14 dc)*

Rnd 2: Ch 3, dc in same st, 2 dc in each st around, join with sl st in 3rd ch of beg ch-3. *(28 dc)*

Rnd 3: Ch 3, dc in same st, *dc in next st, 2 dc in next st, **pc** *(see Special Stitch)* in next st, 2 dc in next st, rep from * around, ending with pc in last st, join with sl st in 3rd ch of beg ch-3. *(7 pcs, 35 dc)*

Rnd 4: Ch 3, dc in same st, dc in each of next 2 sts, 2 dc in next st, rep from * around, ending with dc in each of last 2 sts, join with sl st in 3rd ch of beg ch-3. Fasten off. *(56 dc)*

Assembly & Handle
Holding side WS tog and working through both thicknesses, join with sl st in any st, sl st edges tog leaving 17 sts unworked for top of purse, ch

50 for handle, join with sl st in first sl st. Fasten off.

TOTE BAG
Use 3 colors
Front

Row 1: With first color, ch 24, dc in 4th ch from hook *(first 3 chs count as first dc)* and in each ch across, turn. *(22 dc)*

Row 2: Ch 3, dc in each st across, turn. Fasten off.

Row 3: Join 2nd color with sl st in first st, ch 3, dc in each of next 2 sts, **fptr** *(see Stitch Guide)* around dc 2 rows below, *dc in each of next 2 sts, fptr around dc 2 rows below, rep from * across, dc in each of last 3 sts, turn. Fasten off. *(22 sts)*

Row 4: Join first color with sl st in first st, rep row 2.

Row 5: Join 3rd color with sl st in first st, ch 3, fptr around fptr 2 rows below, *dc in each of next 2 sts, fptr around fptr 2 rows below, rep from * across, dc in each of last 3 sts, turn. Fasten off. *(22 sts)*

Row 6: Join first color with sl st in first st, rep row 2.

Row 7: Rep row 3.

Rows 8 & 9: Rep rows 4 and 5.

Rows 10 & 11: Rep rows 6 and 7.

Row 12: Rep row 4, **do not fasten off.**

Row 13: Ch 1, sc in each st across. Fasten off.

Back

Row 1: Rep row 1 of Front.

Rows 2–10: Ch 3, dc in each st across, turn.

Row 11: Ch 1, sc in each st across. Fasten off.

Assembly & Handle

Holding Front and Back WS tog and working through both thicknesses, join first color with sl st at top left corner, sl st edges tog down side, across bottom and up other side with 5 sc in each bottom corner, at top edge join another strand of first color and working with both strands held tog, ch 43 for handle, sl st in first sl st. Fasten off.

DUFFEL BAG
Use 1 color
End
Make 2.

Rnd 1: Ch 5, sl st in first ch to form ring, ch 3 (counts as first dc), 13 dc in ring, join with sl st in 3rd ch of beg ch-3. (14 dc)

Rnd 2: Ch 3, dc in same st, 2 dc in each st around, join with sl st in 3rd ch of beg ch-3. (28 dc)

Rnd 3: Ch 3, dc in same st, *dc in next st, 2 dc in next st, **pc** (see Special Stitches) in next st, 2 dc in next st, rep from * around, ending with pc in last st, join with sl st in 3rd ch of beg ch-3. Fasten off. (7 pcs, 35 dc)

Side
Row 1: Ch 20, dc in 4th ch from hook (first 3 chs count as first dc) and in each ch across, turn. (18 dc)

Rows 2–27: Ch 3 (counts as first dc), dc in each st across, turn. At end of last row, fasten off.

Assembly & Handle

Holding 1 End circle and 1 long edge of Side WS tog and working through both thicknesses, join with sl st where corner of Side and edge of End meet, sl st edges tog around circle. Fasten off.

For opposite end, rep above, **do not fasten off**, join another strand of yarn and working with both strands held tog, ch 55 for handle, sl st in first sl st at opposite end of bag opening. Fasten off.

SQUARE PURSE
Use 1 color
Row 1: Ch 17, dc in 4th ch from hook (first 3 chs count as first dc) and in each ch across, turn. (15 dc)

Rows 2 & 3: Ch 1, sc in each st across, turn.

Row 4: Ch 3 (counts as first dc), dc in each st across, turn.

Rows 5–18: Rep rows 2–4 consecutively.

Rnd 19: Ch 1, sc in each st across, do not turn, working around outside edge, fold piece across row 6 and working through both thicknesses for side seams and through sts of row 6 for bottom, sc in each st and end of each sc row around with 2 sc in end of each dc row, join with sl st in beg sc.

Rnd 20: Ch 1, *(sc, ch 2, 2 dc) in next st, sk next 2 sts, rep from * around, join with sl st in beg sc. Fasten off.

Strap

Join with sl st in ch-2 sp at end of row 13, ch 44, join with sl st in ch-2 sp at opposite end of row 13. Fold at row 13 for front flap. ❏❏

Stylish Shawls

BLUE SHAWL
Design by Juanita Turner
SKILL LEVEL

EASY

FINISHED SIZE
4 x 9 inches including Fringe

MATERIALS
- ❏ Super fine (fingering) weight yarn: 1 oz/170 yds/28g blue
- ❏ Size G/6/4mm crochet hook or size needed to obtain gauge

GAUGE
6 sc = 1 inch; 6 sc rows = 1 inch

INSTRUCTIONS
SHAWL

Row 1: Starting at upper edge, ch 52, sc in 2nd ch from hook and in each ch across, turn. (51 sc)

Row 2: Ch 1, sc in each of first 11 sc, [hdc in next sc, dc in each of next 2 sc, 2 tr in each of next 2 sc, dc in each of next 2 sc, hdc in next st], sc in each of next 2 sc, hdc in next sc, 2 sc in each of next 2 sc, 2 tr in each of next 3 sc, 2 dc in each of next 2 sc, hdc in next sc, sc in each of next 2 sc, rep between [ ] once, sc in each of last 11 sc, turn. (62 sts)

Row 3: Ch 1, sc in each of first 11 sc, [hdc in next st, dc in each of next 2 sts, 2 tr in each of next 4 sts, dc in each of next 2 sts, hdc in next st], sc in each of next 2 sts, hdc in next st, 2 dc in each of next 4 sts, 2 tr in each of next 6 sts, 2 dc in each of next 4 sts, hdc in next st, sc in each of next 2 sc; rep between [ ] once, sc in each of last 11 sts. Fasten off. (84 sts)

Fringe

Cut 84 strands, each 7 inches long. Fold in half, pull fold through, pull ends through fold.

Place Fringe in each st at scalloped edge. Trim following scalloped shaping.

TEAL SHAWL
Design by Mary Layfield
SKILL LEVEL

EASY

FINISHED SIZE
6 inches across

MATERIALS
- ❏ Fine (sport) weight yarn: 1 oz/90 yds/28g teal
- ❏ Size E/4/3.5mm crochet hook or size needed to obtain gauge
- ❏ Small snap
- ❏ Small decorative button

GAUGE
11 dc = 2 inches

INSTRUCTIONS
SHAWL

Row 1: Starting at neck edge, ch 28, sc in 2nd ch from hook and in each

ch across, turn. *(27 sc)*

Row 2: Ch 2 *(counts as hdc)*, 2 hdc in next sc, dc in next sc, (dc, tr) in next sc, tr in each of next 3 sc, [2 tr in next sc, tr in next sc] 5 times, tr in each of next 2 sc, (tr, dc) in next sc, dc in next sc, 2 hdc in next sc, hdc in next sc, leaving rem 4 sc unworked, turn. *(32 sts)*

Row 3: Ch 2, hdc in same st, dc in each of next 2 sts, 2 dc in next st, [tr in next st, 2 tr in next st] 11 times, tr in next st, 2 dc in next st, dc in next st, 2 hdc in last st, turn, leaving last 2 sts unworked. *(45 sts)*

Row 4: Ch 2, 2 hdc in next st, [dc in next st, 2 dc in next st] 20 times, dc in next st, 2 hdc in next st, hdc in last st, turn. *(67 sts)*

Row 5: Ch 1, sc in each of first 10 sts, (hdc, dc) in next st, tr in each of next 45 sts, (dc, hdc) in next st, sc in each of last 10 sts. Fasten off.

Edging

At extension edge, join with sc in end of row 2, [ch 4, sc in end of next row] 3 times, [ch 4, sc in next sc] across row, [ch 4, sc in end of next row] 4 times. Fasten off.

FINISHING

Sew 1 half of snap to WS of extension and other half at opposite end of row 1.

Sew button to RS of extension.

PEACH SHAWL
Design by Juanita Turner
SKILL LEVEL

EASY

FINISHED SIZE

2½ x 16½ inches

MATERIALS

❏ Super fine (fingering) weight yarn:
   1 oz/170 yds/28g peach

❏ Size G/6/4mm crochet hook or size needed to obtain gauge

GAUGE

10 ch sps = 3 inches; 7 ch sp rows = 2 inches

INSTRUCTIONS
SHAWL

Row 1: Starting at lower edge, ch 114,

BARBIE® and associated trademarks are owned by and used with permission from Mattel, Inc. ©2005 Mattel, Inc.

sc in 2nd ch from hook and in each ch across, turn. *(113 sc)*

Row 2: Ch 4, *(counts as first dc and ch 1)*, [sk next sc, dc in next sc, ch 1] across, dc in last sc, turn. *(56 ch sps)*

Row 3: Ch 4 [dc in next dc, ch 1] across, dc in last dc, turn.

Rows 4–8: Ch 4 [dc in next dc, ch 1] across, dc in last dc, turn. At end of last row, fasten off. ❏❏

Jogging Set

Design by Norma Bonk

SKILL LEVEL

INTERMEDIATE

FINISHED SIZE

Fits 11½-inch fashion doll

MATERIALS

- ❑ Crochet cotton size 20: 350 yds each white and blue
- ❑ Size 5/1.90mm steel crochet hook or size needed to obtain gauge
- ❑ Tapestry needle
- ❑ Sewing needle
- ❑ Sewing thread
- ❑ 3 small snaps *(for Pants)*
- ❑ 5 small buttons *(for Jacket)*

GAUGE

9 sc = 1 inch; 11 sc rows = 1 inch, 4 cls = 1 inch; 4 cl rows = 1 inch

SPECIAL STITCHES

Beginning cluster (beg cl): Ch 3, insert hook in st or sp specified, yo, pull through st or sp, yo, pull through 2 lps on hook, [yo, insert hook in same st or sp, yo, pull through st or sp, yo, pull through 2 lps on hook] twice, yo, pull through all lps on hook.

Cluster (cl): Yo, insert hook in next st or sp specified, yo, pull through st or sp, yo, pull through 2 lps on hook, [yo, insert hook in same st or sp, yo, pull through st or sp, yo, pull through 2 lps on hook] 3 times, yo, pull through all lps on hook.

INSTRUCTIONS
STIRRUP PANTS

Row 1: With blue, ch 25, sc in 2nd ch from hook and in each ch across, turn. *(24 sc)*

Row 2: Ch 1, 2 sc in first st, sc in next st, [2 sc in next st, sc in next st] across, turn. *(36 sc)*

Row 3: Ch 1, sc in each st across, turn.

Row 4: Ch 1, sc in each of first 6 sts, *2 sc in next st, sc in each of next 5

BARBIE® and associated trademarks are owned by and used with permission from Mattel, Inc. ©2005 Mattel, Inc.

sts, 2 sc in next st*, sc in each of next 10 sts; rep between *, sc in each of last 6 sts, turn. *(40 sc)*

Row 5: Ch 1, sc in each st across, turn.

Row 6: Ch 1, sc in each of first 7 sts, *2 sc in next st, sc in each of next 5 sts, 2 sc in next st*, sc in each of next 12 sts; rep between *, sc in each of last 7 sts, turn. *(44 sc)*

Row 7: Ch 1, sc in each st across, turn.

Row 8: Ch 1, sc in each of first 8 sts, *2 sc in next st, sc in each of next 5 sts, 2 sc in next st*, sc in each of next 14 sts; rep between *, sc in each of last 8 sts, turn. *(48 sc)*

Row 9: Ch 1, sc in each st across, turn.

Row 10: Ch 1, sc in each of first 9 sts, *2 sc in next st, sc in each of next 5 sts, 2 sc in next st*, sc in each of next 16 sts; rep between *, sc in each of last 9 sts, turn. *(52 sc)*

Row 11: Ch 1, sc in each st across, turn.

Row 12: Ch 1, sc in each of first 10 sts, *2 sc in next st, sc in each of next 5 sts, 2 sc in next st*, sc in each of next 18 sts; rep between *, sc in each of last 10 sts, turn. *(56 sc)*

Rows 13–18: Ch 1, sc in each st across, turn.

Rnd 19: Working in rnds, ch 1, sc in each st around, join with sl st in beg sc.

First Leg

Rnd 20: Ch 1, sc in each of first 28 sts, join with sl st in beg sc, leaving last 28 sts unworked. *(28 sc)*

Rnd 21: Working in continuous rnds, mark first st of each rnd, sc in each st around.

Rnds 22–32: Sc in each st around.

Rnd 33: Sc dec *(see Stitch Guide)* in first 2 sts, sc in each st across to last 2 sts, sc dec in last 2 sts. *(26 sc)*

Rnds 34–38: Sc in each st around.

Rnd 39: Rep rnd 33. *(24 sc)*

Rnds 40–44: Sc in each st around.

Rnd 45: Rep rnd 33. *(22 sc)*

Rnds 46–61: Sc in each st around.

Rnds 62–66: Rep rnds 33 and 21 alternately ending with rnd 33. *(16 sc at end of rnd 66)*

Rnds 67–70: Sc in each st around. At end of last rnd, join with sl st in beg sc. Fasten off.

Second Leg

Rnd 20: Join blue with sc in next unworked st on rnd 19, sc in each st around, join with sl st in beg sc.

Rnds 21–70: Rep rnds 21–70 of First Leg.

Foot Strap

Row 1: Working in 2 sts on rnd 70 of 1 Leg, beg at instep, join blue with sc in st, sc in next st, turn. *(2 sc)*

Rows 2–12: Ch 1, sc in first 2 sts, turn. At end of last row, fasten off.

With tapestry needle and blue, sew other end of Strap to opposite side.

Rep Foot Strap on other Leg.

Placket

Row 1: Join blue with sc in end of row 1 on Pants, evenly sp 19 more sc down to rnd 19, sl st in joining, evenly sp 20 sc up other side of rows 19–1, turn.

Rows 2 & 3: Ch 1, sc in each of first 20 sc, turn. At end of last row, **do not turn.**

Row 4: Ch 1, sc in end of first 3 rows, working over sts on row 1 at waist, sc in each st across row 2 *(this makes a long sc),* sc in end of row 1 on Placket. Fasten off.

With sewing needle and sewing thread, sew 3 snaps evenly spaced down Placket.

JACKET

Row 1: Starting at waistband, with white, ch 8, sc in 2nd ch from hook and in each ch across, turn. *(7 sc)*

Rows 2–40: Working in **back lps** *(see Stitch Guide)* only, ch 1, sc in each of first 7 sts, turn. At end of last row, fasten off.

Bodice

Row 1: Working in ends of rows on waistband, join blue with sl st in end of row 1, **beg cl** *(see Special Stitches)* in same row as sl st, ch 1, **cl** *(see Special Stitches)* in end of next row, ch 1, sk next row, cl in end of next row, *ch 1, sk next row, (cl, ch 1, cl) in end of next row, [ch 1, sk next row, cl in end of next row] twice; rep from * across, turn. *(26 ch sps)*

Row 2: Ch 4 *(counts as dc and ch 1),* [cl in next ch-1 sp, ch 1] across, ending with dc in 3rd ch of ch-3 of beg cl, turn.

Row 3: Sl st in ch-1 sp, beg cl in same ch-1 sp, [ch 1, cl in next ch-1 sp] across, turn.

Rows 4–8: Rep rows 2 and 3 alternately ending with row 2.

Right Front

Row 9: Sl st in ch-1 sp, beg cl in same ch-1 sp, [ch 1, cl in next ch-1 sp] 4 times, leaving rem ch-1 sps unworked, turn.

Row 10: Ch 4, [cl in next ch-1 sp, ch 1] 4 times, ch 1, dc in top of ch-3 of beg cl, turn.

Rows 11 & 12: Rep rows 9 and 10.

Row 13: Sl st across and into 3rd ch-1 sp, beg cl in same ch-1 sp, [ch 1, cl in next ch-1 sp] 3 times. Fasten off.

Back

Row 9: Working in unworked ch-1 sps on row 8, join blue with sl st in 4th ch-1 sp from Right Front, beg cl in same ch-1 sp, [ch 1, cl in next ch-1 sp] 9 times, leaving rem ch sps unworked, turn.

Row 10: Ch 4, [cl in next ch-1 sp, ch 1] 9 times, dc in 3rd ch of beg ch-3 of beg cl, turn.

Row 11: Sl st in next ch-1 sp, beg cl in same ch-1 sp, [ch 1, cl in next ch-1 sp] across, turn.

Rows 12 & 13: Rep rows 10 and 11. At end of last row, fasten off.

Left Front

Row 9: Working in unworked ch-1 sps on row 8, join blue with sl st in 4th ch-1 sp from Back, beg cl in same ch-1 sp, [ch 1, cl in next ch-1 sp] 4 times, turn.

Rows 10–13: Rep rows 10–13 of Right Front.

With tapestry needle and blue, sew Fronts and Back shoulders tog.

Cuff Ribbing
Make 2.

Row 1: With white, ch 5, sc in 2nd ch from hook and in each ch across, turn. *(4 sc)*

Rows 2–12: Working in back lps only, ch 1, sc in each st across, turn. At end of last row, fasten off.

First Sleeve

Row 1: Join blue with sl st in end of first row on 1 Cuff Ribbing, (beg cl, ch 1, cl) in end of same row, *ch 1, sk next row, (cl, ch 1, cl) in end of next row; rep from * 4 times, sk last row, turn. *(11 ch-1 sps)*

Row 2: Ch 4, [cl in next ch-1 sp, ch 1] across, dc in 3rd ch of beg ch-3 of beg cl, turn.

Row 3: Sl st in ch-1 sp, beg cl in same ch-1 sp, [ch 1, cl in next ch-1 sp] across, turn.

Rows 4–10: Rep rows 2 and 3 alternately ending with row 2.

Row 11: Sl st across and into 3rd ch-1 sp from end, beg cl in same ch-1 sp, [ch 1, cl in next ch-1 sp] 7 times, turn.

Row 12: Sl st into first ch-1 sp, beg cl in same ch-1 sp, [ch 1, cl in next ch-1 sp] 6 times, turn.

Row 13: Sl st into first ch-1 sp, beg cl in same ch sp, [ch 1, cl in next ch-1 sp] 5 times. Fasten off.

Second Sleeve

Rows 1–3: With blue, rep rows 1–3 of First Sleeve.

Row 4: Ch 4, [cl in next ch-1 sp, ch 1] across, dc in top of ch 3 of beg cl, turn. Fasten off.

Row 5: Join white with sl st in ch-1 sp, beg cl in same ch-1 sp, [ch 1, cl in next ch-1 sp] across, turn.

Rows 6 & 7: Rep rows 2 and 3 of First Sleeve. At end of last row, fasten off.

Row 8: Join blue with sl st in first cl, ch 4, [cl in next ch-1 sp, ch 1] across ending with sc in 3rd ch of ch-3 of beg cl, turn.

Rows 9 & 10: Rep rows 3 and 2 of First Sleeve.

Rows 11–13: Rep rows 11–13 of First Sleeve.

With tapestry needle and matching crochet cotton, sew ends of rows on 1 Sleeve tog.

Rep with other Sleeve. Easing to fit, center and sew Sleeves in openings.

Hood

Row 1: Working across neck edge, at top of Bodice on Jacket, join blue with sl st in ch-1 sp at 1 end, beg cl in same ch-1 sp, (ch 1, cl) in ch-1 sp worked evenly across for at total of 21 cls, turn.

Row 2: Ch 4, [cl in next ch-1 sp, ch 1) across ending with sc in 3rd ch of beg ch-3 of beg cl, turn.

Row 3: Sl st in ch-1 sp, beg cl in same ch-1 sp, [ch 1, cl in next ch-1 sp] across, turn.

Rows 4–11: Rep rows 2 and 3 alternately. At end of last row, fasten off.

Fold Hood in half, with tapestry needle and blue, sew sts tog for top.

Front Edging & Trim

Row 1: Join white with sl st at bottom

Right Front edge, evenly sp 30 sc across to Hood, evenly sp 42 sc across Hood, evenly sp 30 sc across to bottom edge on other Front, turn. *(102 sc)*

Row 2: Ch 1, sc in each st across, turn.

Row 3: Ch 1, sc in each of first 3 sts; for **buttonhole**, [ch 2, sk next 2 sc, sc in each of next 4 sts] 4 times, ch 2, sk next 2 sc, sc in each st across, turn.

Row 4: Ch 1, sc in each of first 30 sc, turn.

Row 5: Ch 1, sc in each of first 30 sts. Fasten off.

Row 4: Working on other side, in rem sts and chs, join with sc in first st, sc in each of last 29 sts, turn.

Row 5: Ch 1, sc in each of first 30 sts. Fasten off.

With sewing needle and sewing thread, sew 1 button opposite each buttonhole. ❑❑

Evening Out

Designs by Elizabeth White

DRESS & JACKET

SKILL LEVEL

INTERMEDIATE

FINISHED SIZE
Fits 11½-inch fashion doll

MATERIALS
❑ Fine (sport) weight acrylic yarn: 110 yds black
❑ Size 0/2.50mm steel crochet hook or size needed to obtain gauge
❑ Embroidery needle
❑ 3 small snaps

GAUGE
11 dc = 2 inches; 3 dc rows = 1 inch

INSTRUCTIONS
DRESS
Skirt
Row 1: Ch 25, dc in 4th ch from hook and in each ch across, turn. *(23 dc)*

Rnd 2: Working in rnds, ch 3 *(counts as first dc)*, dc in same st, [dc in each of next 2 sts, 2 dc in next st] around to last st, dc in last st, join with sl st in top of beg ch-3. *(31 dc)*

Rnds 3–11: Ch 3, dc in each st around, join with sl st in 3rd ch of beg ch-3. At end of last rnd, fasten off.

Bodice
Row 1: Working in starting ch on opposite side of row 1 on Skirt, join with sl st in first ch, ch 3, dc in each ch across, turn. *(23 dc)*

Row 2: Ch 3, dc in same st, [dc in each of next 2 sts, 2 dc in next st] across to last st, dc in last st, turn. *(31 dc)*

BARBIE® and associated trademarks are owned by and used with permission from Mattel, Inc. ©2005 Mattel, Inc.

Rows 3 & 4: Ch 3, dc in each st across, turn.

First Back Side
Row 5: Ch 3, dc in each of next 4 sts leaving rem sts unworked, turn.

Row 6: Ch 3, dc in each st across, turn.

Row 7: Sl st in each of first 3 sts, ch 3,

dc in each of last 2 sts. Fasten off.

Second Back Side
Row 5: Join with sc in first st at opposite end of row 4, sc in each of next 4 sts, turn.

Row 6: Ch 3, dc in each st across, turn.

Row 7: Sl st in each of first 3 sts, ch 3, dc in each of last 2 sts. Fasten off.

Front
Row 5: Sk next 3 unworked sts on row 4, join with sl st in next st, ch 3, dc in each of next 14 sts leaving rem sts unworked, turn.
Row 6: Ch 3, dc in each st across, turn.
Row 7: For **first shoulder**, ch 3, dc in each of next 2 sts leaving rem sts unworked. Fasten off.
Row 7: For **2nd shoulder**, join with sl st in first st on opposite side of row 6, ch 3, dc in each of next 2 sts leaving rem sts unworked. Fasten off.
Sew shoulder seams.

Placket
Join with sl st in end of last row on back opening, ch 3, evenly sp 19 dc down opening. Fasten off.

JACKET
Row 1: Ch 35, dc in 4th ch from hook and in each ch across, turn. *(33 dc)*
Rows 2–4: Ch 3, dc in each st across, turn.

First Front Side
Row 5: Ch 3, dc in each of next 7 sts leaving rem sts unworked, turn.
Rows 6 & 7: Ch 3, dc in each st across, turn.
Row 8: Ch 3, dc in each of next 3 sts leaving rem sts unworked. Fasten off.

Second Front Side
Row 5: Join with sl st in first st on opposite side of row 4, ch 3, dc in each of next 8 sts leaving rem sts unworked, turn.
Rows 6 & 7: Ch 3, dc in each st across, turn.
Row 8: Ch 3, dc in each of next 3 sts. Fasten off.

Back
Row 5: Sk next 3 sts on row 4, join with sl st in next st, ch 3, dc in each of next 10 sts, turn leaving rem sts unworked. *(10 dc)*
Rows 6 & 7: Ch 3, dc in each st across, turn.

First Shoulder
Row 8: Ch 3, dc in each of next 3 sts leaving rem sts unworked. Fasten off.

Second Shoulder
Row 8: Join with sl st in first st at opposite end of row 7, ch 3, dc in next 3 sts. Fasten off.
Sew shoulder seams.

Sleeve
Rnd 1: Join with sl st in first skipped st on row 4, ch 3, evenly sp 14 dc around, join with sl st in 3rd ch of beg ch-3.
Rnds 2–9: Ch 3, dc in each st around, join with sl st in 3rd ch of beg ch-3. At end of last rnd, fasten off.
Rep on rem armhole.

SHAWL & PURSE
SKILL LEVEL

INTERMEDIATE

FINISHED SIZE
Fits 11½-inch fashion doll

MATERIALS
❑ Metallic crochet cotton size 10: 110 yds gold
❑ Size 3/2.10mm and 7/1.65mm steel crochet hooks

INSTRUCTIONS
SHAWL
Row 1: With size 7 hook, ch 20, dc in 6th ch from hook, [ch 1, sk next ch, dc in next ch] across, turn.
Row 2: Ch 3, dc in each st and in each ch across, turn. *(17 dc)*
Rows 3–29: Ch 3, dc in each st across, turn.
Row 30: Ch 4, sk next st, dc in next st, [ch 1, sk next st, dc in next st) across. Fasten off.

Fringe
Cut 5 strands of thread each 6 inches long, fold in half, insert hook in ch sp, pull fold through, pull ends through fold, tighten.
Fringe in ch sps across ends.

PURSE
Rnd 1: With size 3 hook, ch 4, 11 dc in 4th ch from hook *(first 3 chs count as first dc)*, join with sl st in 4th ch of beg ch-4.
Rnd 2: Working in **back lps** *(see Stitch Guide)*, ch 3 *(counts as first dc)*, dc in each st around, join with sl st in 3rd ch of beg ch-3.
Rnd 3: Ch 3, dc in each st around, join with sl st in 3rd ch of beg ch-3.
Rnd 4: Ch 4 *(counts as first dc and ch 1)*, sk next st, [dc in next st, ch 1, sk next st] around, join with sl st in 3rd ch of ch-4.
Rnd 5: (Sl st, sc, ch 1, 2 dc) in first ch sp, (sc, ch 1, 2 dc) in each ch sp around, join with sl st in beg sc. Fasten off.

Drawstring
Make 2.
Ch 40. Fasten off.
Beg and ending on 1 side of Purse, weave 1 drawstring through ch sps on rnd 4, tie ends tog. Rep on opposite side of Purse with 2nd drawstring.

PANTS & BLOUSE
SKILL LEVEL
INTERMEDIATE

FINISHED SIZE
Fits 11½-inch fashion doll

MATERIALS
❑ Fine (sport) weight acrylic yarn: 80 yds black 55 yds white
❑ Size 0/2.50mm steel crochet hook or size needed to obtain gauge
❑ Embroidery needle
❑ Sewing needle
❑ Sewing thread
❑ 4 small snaps

GAUGE
11 dc = 2 inches; 3 dc rows = 1 inch

INSTRUCTIONS
PANTS
Row 1: With black, ch 26, dc in 4th ch from hook and in each ch across, turn. *(24 dc)*
Row 2: Ch 3 *(counts as first dc)*, dc in same st, [dc in each of next 2 sts, 2 dc in next st] across to last 2 sts, dc in each of last 2 sts, turn. *(32 dc)*
Rows 3 & 4: Ch 3, dc in each st across, turn.

First Leg
Rnd 5: Working in rnds, ch 3, dc in each of next 15 sts, ch 4, join with sl st in 3rd ch of beg ch-3.

Rnd 6: Ch 3, dc in each st and in each ch around, join with sl st in 3rd ch of beg ch-3.

Rnds 7–19: Ch 3, dc in each st around, join with sl st in 3rd ch of beg ch-3. At end of last rnd, fasten off.

Second Leg

Rnd 5: Join black with sl st in first unworked st on row 4, ch 3, dc in each st and in each ch around, join with sl st in 3rd ch of beg ch-3.

Rnds 6–19: Ch 3, dc in each st around, join with sl st in 3rd ch of beg ch-3. At end of last rnd, fasten off.

Placket

Join black with sl st at top of back opening, ch 3, evenly sp 4 dc down opening. Fasten off.

Sew 1 snap to placket. Sew crotch seam.

BLOUSE

Row 1: With white, ch 35, dc in 4th ch from hook and in each ch across, turn. *(33 dc)*

Rows 2–4: Ch 3, dc in each st across, turn.

First Shoulder

Row 5: Ch 3, dc in each of next 7 sts leaving rem sts unworked, turn. *(8 dc)*

Rows 6 & 7: Ch 3, dc in each st across, turn.

Row 8: Ch 3, dc in each of next 3 sts leaving rem sts unworked. Fasten off.

Second Shoulder

Row 5: Join white with sl st in first st at opposite end of row 4, ch 3, dc in each of next 7 sts leaving rem sts unworked, turn. *(8 dc)*

Rows 6 & 7: Ch 3, dc in each st across, turn.

Row 8: Ch 3, dc in each of next 3 sts leaving rem sts unworked. Fasten off.

Back

Row 5: Sk next 3 unworked sts on row 4, join white with sl st in next st, ch 3, dc in each of next 10 sts leaving rem sts unworked, turn. *(10 dc)*

Rows 6 & 7: Ch 3, dc in each st across, turn.

First Shoulder

Row 8: Ch 3, dc in each of next 3 sts leaving rem sts unworked. Fasten off.

Second Shoulder

Row 8: Join white with sl st in first st at opposite end of row 7, ch 3, dc in each of next 3 sts leaving rem sts unworked. Fasten off.

Sew shoulder seams.

Sleeve

Rnd 1: Join white with sl st in first skipped st on row 4, ch 3, evenly sp 14 dc around, join with sl st in 3rd ch of beg ch-3.

Rnds 2–4: Ch 3, dc in each st around, join with sl st in 3rd ch of beg ch-3.

Rnd 5: Ch 1, sc in each st around, join with sl st in beg sc. Fasten off.

Rep on rem armhole.

Sew snaps evenly spaced down back opening. ❑❑

Afternoon Tea Party

Designs by Kathleen Rizzs

LOVE SEAT

SKILL LEVEL

◼◼◼▢

INTERMEDIATE

FINISHED SIZE
2½ inches high x 3¾ inches wide

MATERIALS
- ❑ Crochet cotton size 10: 50 yds white
- ❑ Size 7/1.65mm steel crochet hook or size needed to obtain gauge
- ❑ 4 white ¾-inch oval plastic beads
- ❑ White chenille stem
- ❑ Scrap of 1-inch-thick plastic foam
- ❑ Plastic wrap
- ❑ Fabric stiffener
- ❑ Straight pins
- ❑ Fabric glue
- ❑ Small brush

GAUGE

8 sc = 1 inch; 9 sc rows = 1 inch

INSTRUCTIONS

LOVE SEAT

Seat

Row 1: Ch 20, sc in 2nd ch from hook and in each ch across, turn. *(19 sc)*

Rows 2–7: Ch 1, sc in each sc across, turn.

Row 8: Ch 1, 2 sc in first sc, sc in each of next 17 sc, 2 sc in last sc, mark last sc. **Do not fasten off.** *(21 sc)*

Row 9: Ch 1, evenly sp 6 sc along side edge to next corner, 2 sc in first sc in beg edge, sc in each of next 17 sc, 2 sc in next sc, sc in side edge, mark this sc, evenly sp 5 more sc on side edge, join with sl st in first sc at beg of row 8. **Do not fasten off.**

Back

Row 1: Working in **front lps** *(see Stitch Guide)* only, [ch 5, sk next sc, sc in next sc] 9 times, ch 2, sk next sc, dc in next sc, turn. *(10 ch sps)*

Row 2: [Ch 5, sl st in 3rd ch of next ch sp] 8 times, ch 2, sk next sc, dc in 3rd ch of next ch sp, turn. *(9 ch sps)*

Row 3: [Ch 5, sl st in 3rd ch of next ch sp] 7 times, ch 2, sk next sc, dc in 3rd ch of next ch sp, turn. *(8 ch sps)*

Row 4: [Ch 5, sl st in 3rd ch of next ch sp] 6 times, ch 2, sk next sc, dc in 3rd ch of next ch sp, turn. *(7 ch sps)*

Row 5: [Ch 5, sl st in 3rd ch of next ch sp] 5 times, ch 5, sl st in next ch sp. Fasten off.

Arms & Scallop Edging

Row 1: With front of Love Seat facing, sl st in marked sc at left arm, ch 5, sk next 2 sc, dc in front lp of next sc, ch 5, sl st in first ch sp on row 1 of Back, working around Back, [ch 5, sc in next ch sp] 3 times, [ch 5, sc in next sl st] 6 times, [ch 5, sc in next ch sp] 3 times, ch 5, sk next 2 sc, dc in front lp of next sc, ch 5, sk next 2 sc, sl st in next sc. Fasten off.

Row 2: Join with sl st in same sl st at beg of row 1, ch 1, sc in sl st, (sc, hdc, dc, hdc, sc) in each ch sp around, sc in last sl st. Fasten off.

Bottom Skirt

Rnd 1: Working in back lps on last row of Seat, sl st in sc at right front corner, [ch 5, sk next 2 sc, sc in next sc] 17 times, ch 2, sk next 2 sc, dc in beg sl st.

Rnd 2: [Ch 4, sl st in 3rd ch of next ch sp] around, sl st at base of beg ch-4.

Rnd 3: (Sl st, ch 1, 2 sc, sl st) in each ch sp around, join with sl st in beg sl st. Fasten off.

Finishing

Cut foam piece the same size as seat. Cover with plastic wrap. Place Love Seat over foam and pin in place. Brush with stiffener. While still damp, shape Love Seat. Brush on a 2nd coat of stiffener. Allow to dry completely. Remove pins and foam.

Legs

Cut 2 pieces of chenille stem each 3 inches in length. Bend each in a "U" shape to make 2 legs, each 1 inch. Glue each under seat. Coat each leg with glue, and thread an oval bead on each leg *(see illustration)*. Adjust stems as necessary to be level.

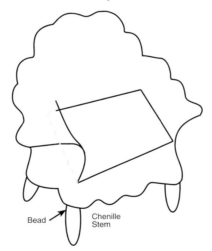

Bead    Chenille Stem

CHAIR

SKILL LEVEL

■ ■ ■ ▢

INTERMEDIATE

FINISHED SIZE

2½ inches high

MATERIALS

- ❑ Crochet cotton size 10:
     50 yds white
- ❑ Size 7/1.65mm steel crochet hook or size needed to obtain gauge
- ❑ 8 white ¾-inch oval plastic beads
- ❑ White chenille stem
- ❑ Scraps of 1-inch-thick plastic foam
- ❑ Plastic wrap
- ❑ Fabric stiffener
- ❑ Straight pins
- ❑ Fabric glue
- ❑ Small brush

GAUGE

8 sc = 1 inch; 9 sc rows = 1 inch

INSTRUCTIONS

CHAIR

Make 2.

Seat

Row 1: Starting at seat, ch 10, sc in 2nd ch from hook and in each ch across, turn. *(9 sc)*

Rows 2–7: Ch 1, sc in each sc across, turn.

Row 8: Ch 1, 2 sc in first sc, sc in each of next 7 sc, 2 sc in last sc, mark last sc. **Do not turn or fasten off.** *(11 sc)*

Row 9: Ch 1, evenly sp 6 sc along side edge to next corner, 2 sc in first sc in beg edge, sc in each of next 7 sc, 2 sc in next sc, sc in side edge, mark this sc, evenly sp 5 more sc on side edge, sl st in first sc at beg of row 8. **Do not fasten off.**

Back

Row 1: Working in **front lps** *(see Stitch Guide)* only, [ch 5, sk next sc, sc in next sc] 4 times, ch 2, sk next sc, dc in next sc, turn. *(5 ch sps)*

Row 2: [Ch 5, sl st in 3rd ch of next ch sp] 3 times, ch 2, dc in 3rd ch of next ch sp, turn. *(4 ch sps)*

Row 3: [Ch 5, sl st in 3rd ch of next ch sp] twice, ch 2, dc in 3rd ch of next ch sp, turn. *(3 ch sps)*

Row 4: Ch 5, sl st in 3rd ch of next ch sp, ch 2, dc in 3rd ch of next ch sp, turn. *(2 ch sps)*

Row 5: Ch 5, sl st in 3rd ch of next ch sp. Fasten off.

Arms & Scallop Edging

Row 1: With front of Chair facing you, sl st in marked sc at left arm, ch 5, sk next 2 sc, dc in front lp of next sc, ch 5, sl st in first ch sp on row 1 of Back, working around Back, [ch 5, sc in top next ch sp] 3 times, ch

5, sk last ch sp at top of Back, [sc in next ch sp, ch 5] 3 times, sc in next ch sp, ch 5, sk next 2 sc, dc in front lp of next sc, ch 5, sk next 2 sc, sl st in next sc. Fasten off.

Row 2: Sl st in same sl st at beg of row 1, ch 1, sc in sl st, (sc, hdc, dc, hdc, sc) in each ch sp across, sc in last sl st. Fasten off.

Bottom Skirt
Rnd 1: Working in **back lps** (see Stitch Guide) on last row of Seat, sl st in sc at right front corner, [ch 5, sk next 2 sc, sc in next sc] 10 times, ch 2, sk next 2 sc, dc in beg sl st to form last ch sp.

Rnd 2: [Ch 4, sl st in 3rd ch of next ch sp) around, sl st at base of beg ch-4.

Rnd 3: (Sl st, ch 1, 2 sc, sl st) in each ch sp around, sl st in beg sl st. Fasten off.

Finishing
Cut foam piece the same size as seat. Cover with plastic wrap. Place chair over foam and pin in place. Brush with stiffener. While still damp, shape chair. Brush on a 2nd coat of stiffener. Allow to dry completely. Remove pins and foam.

Legs
Cut 2 chenille stems each 3 inches in length. Bend each in a "U" shape to make 2 legs, each 1 inch. Glue each under seat. Coat each leg with glue, and thread an oval bead on each leg (see illustration). Adjust stems as necessary to be level.

FLOWER PLANTER
SKILL LEVEL

INTERMEDIATE

FINISHED SIZE
2 inches long

MATERIALS
- ❑ Crochet cotton size 10:
    25 yds white
- ❑ Size 7/1.65mm steel crochet hook or size needed to obtain gauge
- ❑ 2 white ¼-inch pony beads
- ❑ Small paper flowers
- ❑ Scraps of 1-inch-thick plastic foam
- ❑ Plastic wrap
- ❑ Fabric stiffener
- ❑ Straight pins
- ❑ Fabric glue
- ❑ Small brush

GAUGE
8 sc = 1 inch; 9 sc rows = 1 inch

INSTRUCTIONS
PLANTER
Bottom
Row 1: Ch 14, sc in 2nd ch from hook and in each ch across, turn. (13 sc)

Rows 2 & 3: Ch 1, sc in each sc across, turn.

Row 4: Ch 1, 2 sc in first sc, sc in each of next 11 sc, 2 sc in last sc, mark this sc. **Do not fasten off.** (15 sc)

Row 5: Ch 1, evenly sp 4 sc along side edge to next corner, 2 sc in first sc in beg edge, sc in each of next 11 sc, 2 sc in next sc, sc in side edge, mark this sc, evenly sp 4 more sc on side edge, sl st to first sc at beg of row 4, **do not turn**.

Rnd 6: Ch 1, working in **front lps** (see Stitch Guide) only, sc in each sc around, join with sl st in beg sc. (39 sc)

Rnd 7: [Ch 5, sk next 2 sc, sc in next sc] 12 times, ch 2, dc in base of beg ch-5 to form ch sp. (13 ch sps)

Rnd 8: [Ch 4, sl st in 3rd ch of next ch sp] around, ch 4, sl st at base of beg ch-4.

Rnd 9: (Sl st, ch 1, 2 sc, sl st) in each ch sp around, sl st in beg sl st. Fasten off.

Finishing
Cut foam piece the same size as Planter. Cover with plastic wrap, insert foam piece in Planter, pin in place and brush with stiffener. Allow to dry. Remove pins and foam. Glue 1 pony bead at each end of bottom for legs. Glue flowers inside Planter.

PILLOW
SKILL LEVEL

EASY

FINISHED SIZE
⅞ inch in diameter.

MATERIALS
- ❑ Crochet cotton size 10:
    Small amount pink
- ❑ Size 7/1.65mm steel crochet hook or size needed to obtain gauge
- ❑ Embroidery needle

GAUGE
8 sc = 1 inch; 9 sc rows = 1 inch

INSTRUCTIONS
PILLOW
Front
Rnd 1: With pink, ch 4, 11 dc in 4th ch from hook (first 3 chs count as first dc), join with sl st in 3rd ch of ch-3. (12 dc)

Rnd 2: Working in **back lps** (see Stitch Guide) only, [ch 3, sl st in next dc] around, ch 3, join with sl st in beg sl st. Fasten off.

Back
With pink, ch 4, 11 dc in 4th ch from hook, join with sl st in 3rd ch of beg ch-3. Fasten off.

Button
Ch 4, sl st in 4th ch from hook. Fasten off.

Sew to center Front.

Sew Front to Back, stuffing with leftover thread in same color.

HAT
SKILL LEVEL

EASY

FINISHED SIZE
2½ inches high

MATERIALS
- ❑ Crochet cotton size 10:
    Small amount pink
- ❑ Size 7/1.65mm steel crochet hook or size needed to obtain gauge
- ❑ Embroidery needle
- ❑ 2 pieces of ¼-inch-wide ribbon 4-inches in length

GAUGE
8 sc = 1 inch; 9 sc rows = 1 inch

INSTRUCTIONS
HAT
Make 2.
Rnd 1: With pink, ch 3, 7 hdc in 3rd ch from hook (first 2 chs count as

first hdc), join with sl st in 2nd ch of ch-2. *(8 hdc)*

Rnd 2: Ch 1, working in **front lps** *(see Stitch Guide)* this rnd only, sc in each st around, join with sl st in beg sc.

Rnd 3: Ch 1, working in both lps, sc in each st around, join with sl st in beg sc.

Rnd 4: [Ch 3, sl st in next st] around, ch 3, join with sl st in base of beg ch 3.

Rnd 5: [Ch 4, sc in next sc on rnd 3] around. Fasten off.

Make small bow with ribbon and glue to Hat brim.

TABLE

SKILL LEVEL

INTERMEDIATE

FINISHED SIZE

1½ inches high x 2½ inches across

MATERIALS

- ❏ Crochet cotton size 10: 50 yds white
- ❏ Size 7/1.65mm steel crochet hook or size needed to obtain gauge
- ❏ 4 white ¾-inch oval plastic beads
- ❏ 5 white pony beads
- ❏ White chenille stem
- ❏ Scrap of 1-inch-thick plastic foam
- ❏ Plastic wrap
- ❏ Fabric stiffener
- ❏ Straight pins
- ❏ Fabric glue
- ❏ Small brush

GAUGE

8 sc = 1 inch; 9 sc rows = 1 inch

INSTRUCTIONS

TABLE

Top

Rnd 1: Ch 4, 11 dc in 4th ch from hook *(first 3 chs count as first dc)*, join with sl st in 3rd ch of beg ch-3. *(12 dc)*

Rnd 2: Ch 3, dc in same st, 2 dc in each st around, join with sl st in 3rd ch of beg ch-3. *(24 dc)*

Rnd 3: Ch 3, [dc in next st, 2 dc in next st] around, join with sl st in top of beg ch-3. *(36 dc)*

Rnd 4: Rep rnd 2. *(72 dc)*

Rnd 5: Ch 1, working in **front lps** *(see Stitch Guide)* for this rnd only, sc in each st around, join with sl st in beg sc.

Rnd 6: [Ch 5, sk next 2 sc, sc in next sc] 23 times, ch 2, dc in base of beg ch-5. *(24 ch sps)*

Rnd 7: [Ch 4, sl st in next ch sp] around, sl st in base of beg ch-4.

Rnd 8: (Sl st, ch 1, 2 sc, sl st) in each ch sp around, join with sl st in beg sl st. Fasten off.

Finishing

Place Table overl plastic foam of matching size. Brush with stiffener. Shape and pin in place. Allow to dry completely. Remove pins and foam.

Legs

Cut 4 chenille stems each 3½ inches in length. Holding all 4 tog, thread 5 pony beads onto stems. Bend about ¾ inch back at a 90-degree angle and in a + shape on each end of stems. Coat 1 end of each leg with glue and thread one oval bead in each leg. Glue other bent end to underside of Table *(see Illustration)*. Adjust as necessary to be level. ❏❏

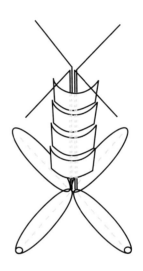

Feather Fantasy

Design by Dell LaSart

SKILL LEVEL

INTERMEDIATE

FINISHED SIZE

Fits 11½-inch fashion doll

MATERIALS

- ❑ Crochet cotton size 10: 700 yds cardinal
- ❑ Size 7/1.65mm steel hook or size needed to obtain gauge
- ❑ Beading needle
- ❑ Sewing needle
- ❑ Dark red sewing thread
- ❑ 60 dark red 1–3-inch craft feathers
- ❑ 3 small snaps
- ❑ 285 gold seed beads
- ❑ Stitch markers

GAUGE

8 sts = 1 inch; 9 sc rows = 1 inch; 3 dc rows = 1 inch

INSTRUCTIONS

DRESS
Bodice

Row 1: Starting at neckline, ch 66, sc in 2nd ch from hook and in each of next 31 chs, 5 sc in next ch, sc in each of last 32 chs, turn. *(69 sc)*

Row 2: Working in **front lps** (see Stitch Guide), ch 1, sc in each of first 34 sts, 3 sc in next st, sc in each of last 34 sts, turn. *(71 sc)*

Row 3: Working in both lps, ch 1, sc in each of first 35 sts, 3 sc in next st, sc in each of last 35 sts, turn. *(73 sc)*

Row 4: Ch 1, sc in each of first 12 sts, for **shoulder**, ch 4, sk next 8 sts, sc in each of next 16 sts, 3 sc in next st, sc in each of next 16 sts, for **shoulder**, ch 4, sk next 8 sts, sc in each of last 12 sts, turn.

Row 5: Ch 1, sc in each of first 12 sts, sc in each of next 4 chs, sc in each of next 17 sts, 3 sc in next st, sc in each of next 17 sts, sc in each of next 4 chs, sc in each of last 12 sts, turn. *(69 sc)*

Row 6: Ch 1, sc in each of first 4 sts, **sc dec** *(see Stitch Guide)* in next 2 sts, [sc in each of next 4 sts, sc dec in next

BARBIE® and associated trademarks are owned by and used with permission from Mattel, Inc. ©2005 Mattel, Inc.

2 sts] 4 times, sc in each of next 9 sts, [sc dec in next 2 sts, sc in each of next 4 sts] across, turn. *(59 sc)*

Row 7: Ch 1, sc in each of first 3 sts, sc dec in next 2 sts, [sc in each of next 3 sts, sc dec in next 2 sts] 4 times, sc in each of next 9 sts, [sc dec in next 2 sts, sc in each of next 3 sts] across, turn. *(49 sc)*

Row 8: Ch 1, sc in each of first 2 sts, sc dec in next 2 sts, [sc in each of next 2 sts, sc dec in next 2 sts] across to last st, 2 sc in last st, turn. *(38 sc)*

Rows 9–14: Ch 1, sc in each st across, turn.

Row 15: Ch 1, sc in each of first 2 sts, [sc dec in next 2 sts, sc in each of next 4 sts] across, turn. *(32 sc)*

Row 16: Ch 1, sc in each of first 2 sts, [sc dec in next 2 sts, sc in each of next 3 sts] across, turn. *(26 sc)*

Rows 17 & 18: Ch 1, sc in each st across, turn.

Skirt

Row 19: Ch 3 *(counts as first dc)*, [2 dc in next st, dc in next st] across, turn. *(39 dc)*

Row 20: Working in front lps, ch 3, dc in each st across, turn.

Rnd 21: Working in rnds and in both lps, ch 3, dc in each of next 11 sts, 2 dc in next st, [dc in each of next 12 sts, 2 dc in next st] twice, join with sl st in top of ch-3. *(42 dc)*

Rnd 22: Ch 3, dc in each st around, join with sl st in 3rd ch of beg ch-3.

Rnd 23: Ch 3, dc in each of next 5 sts, 2 dc in next st, [dc in each of next 6 sts, 2 dc in next st] around, join with sl st in 3rd ch of beg ch-3. *(48 dc)*

Rnds 24–26: Ch 3, dc in each st around, join with sl st in 3rd ch of beg ch-3.

Rnd 27: Ch 3, dc in each of next 6 sts, 2 dc in next st, [dc in each of next 7 sts, 2 dc in next st] around, join with sl st in 3rd ch of beg ch-3. *(54 dc)*

Rnd 28: Ch 3, dc in each of next 7 sts, 2 dc in next st, [dc in each of next 8 sts, 2 dc in next st] around, join with sl st in 3rd ch of beg ch-3. *(60 dc)*

Rnd 29: Ch 3, dc in each of next 8 sts, 2 dc in next st, [dc in each of next 9 sts, 2 dc in next st] around, join with sl st in 3rd ch of beg ch-3. *(66 dc)*

Rnd 30: Ch 3, dc in each of next 9 sts, 2 dc in next st, [dc in each of next 10 sts, 2 dc in next st] around, join with sl st in 3rd ch of beg ch-3. *(72 dc)*

Rnd 31: Ch 3, dc in each of next 4 sts, 3 dc in next st, [dc in each of next 5 sts, 3 dc in next st] around, join with sl st in 3rd ch of beg ch-3. *(96 dc)*

Rnd 32: Ch 3, dc in each of next 5 sts, 3 dc in next st, [dc in each of next 7 sts, 3 dc in next st] around to last st, dc in last st, join with sl st in 3rd ch of beg ch-3. *(120 dc)*

Rnd 33: Ch 3, dc in each of next 6 sts, 3 dc in next st, [dc in each of next 9 sts, 3 dc in next st] around to last 2 sts, dc in each of last 2 sts, join with sl st in 3rd ch of beg ch-3. *(144 dc)*

Rnd 34: Ch 3, dc in each of next 7 sts, 3 dc in next st, [dc in each of next 11 sts, 3 dc in next st] around to last 3 sts, dc in each of last 3 sts, join with sl st in 3rd ch of beg ch-3. *(168 dc)*

Rnd 35: Ch 3, dc in each of next 8 sts, 3 dc in next st, [dc in each of next 13 sts, 3 dc in next st] around to last 4 sts, dc in each of last 4 sts, join with sl st in 3rd ch of beg ch-3. *(192 dc)*

Rnd 36: Working in front lps, ch 3, dc in each of next 9 sts, 3 dc in next st, [dc in each of next 15 sts, 3 dc in next st] around to last 5 sts, dc in

BARBIE® and associated trademarks are owned by and used with permission from Mattel, Inc. ©2005 Mattel, Inc.

each of last 5 sts, join with sl st in 3rd ch of beg ch-3. *(216 dc)*

Rnd 37: Working in both lps, ch 3, 2 dc in same st, dc in each of next 8 sts, [3 dc in next st, dc in each of next 8 sts] around, join with sl st in 3rd ch of beg ch-3. *(264 dc)*

Rnd 38: Ch 3, 2 dc in same st, [dc in each of next 10 sts, 3 dc in next st] around to last 10 sts, dc in each of last 10 sts, join with sl st in 3rd ch of beg ch-3. *(312 dc)*

Rnd 39: Ch 3, dc in each st around, join with sl st in 3rd ch of beg ch-3.

Rnd 40: Working in **back lps** *(see stitch guide)*, ch 3, dc in each st around, join with sl st in 3rd ch of beg ch-3.

Rnd 41: Working in back lps, ch 1, sc in each st around, join with sl st in beg sc.

Rnd 42: Working in both lps, ch 1, sc in each st around, join with sl st in beg sc. Fasten off.

Train

Row 1: With bottom of Skirt facing, working in rem back lps of row 19, join with sl st in 7th st from right back edge, ch 3, 2 dc in same st, 3 dc in each of next 6 sts, 3 dc in each of next 7 sts on left back side, turn. *(42 dc)*

Row 2: Working in back lps, ch 3, dc in each st across, turn.

Row 3: Working in both lps, ch 3, dc in each of next 5 sts, 2 dc in next st, [dc in each of next 6 sts, 2 dc in next st] across to last 7 sts, dc in each of next 5 dc, **dc dec** *(see Stitch Guide)* in last 2 sts, turn. *(46 dc)*

Row 4: Ch 3, dc in each of next 6 sts, 2 dc in next st, [dc in each of next 7 sts, 2 dc in next st] across to last 6 sts, dc in each of last 6 sts, turn. *(51 dc)*

Row 5: Ch 3, dc in each of next 6 sts, 2 dc in next st, [dc in each of next 8 sts, 2 dc in next st] across to last 7 sts, dc in each of last 7 sts, turn. *(56 dc)*

Row 6: Ch 3, dc in each of next 7 sts, 2 dc in next st, [dc in each of next 9 sts, 2 dc in next st] across to last 7 sts, dc in each of last 7 sts, turn. *(61 dc)*

Row 7: Ch 3, dc in each of next 7 sts, 2 dc in next st, [dc in each of next 10 sts, 2 dc in next st] across to last 8 sts, dc in each of last 8 sts, turn. *(66 dc)*

Row 8: Ch 3, dc in each of next 8 sts, 3 dc in next st, [dc in each of next 5 dc, 3 dc in next st] across to last 8 sts, dc in each of last 8 sts, turn. *(84 dc)*

Row 9: Ch 3, dc in each of next 8 sts, 3 dc in next st, [dc in each of next 7 sts, 3 dc in next st] across to last 10 sts, dc in each of last 10 sts, turn. *(102 dc)*

Row 10: Ch 3, dc in each of next 10 sts, 3 dc in next st, [dc in each of next 9 sts, 3 dc in next st] across to last 10 sts, dc in each of last 10 sts, turn. *(120 dc)*

Row 11: Ch 3, dc in each of next 10 sts, 3 dc in next dc, [dc in each of next 11 dc, 3 dc in next dc] across to last 12 sts, dc in each of last 12 sts, turn. *(138 dc)*

Row 12: Ch 3, dc in each of next 12 sts, 3 dc in next st, [dc in each of next 13 sts, 3 dc in next st] across to last 12 sts, dc in each of last 12 sts, turn. *(156 dc)*

Row 13: Ch 3, dc in each of next 4 sts, 3 dc in next st, [dc in each of next 7 sts, 3 dc in next st] across to last 6 sts, dc in each of last 6 sts, turn. *(194 dc)*

Row 14: Ch 3, dc in each of next 6 sts, 3 dc in next st, [dc in each of next 9 sts, 3 dc in next st] across to last 6 sts, dc in each of last 6 sts, turn. *(232 dc)*

Row 15: Ch 3, dc in each of next 6 sts, 3 dc in next st, [dc in each of next 11 sts, 3 dc in next st] across to last 8 sts, dc in each of last 8 sts, turn. *(270 dc)*

Row 16: Ch 3, dc in each of next 8 sts, 3 dc in next st, [dc in each of next 13 sts, 3 dc in next st] across to last 8 sts, dc in each of last 8 sts, turn. *(308 dc)*

Row 17: Ch 3, dc in each of next 8 sts, 3 dc in next dc, [dc in each of next 7 sts, 3 dc in next st] across to last 10 sts, dc in each of last 10 sts, turn. *(382 dc)*

Row 18: Ch 3, dc in each of next 10 sts, 3 dc in next st, [dc in each of next 9 sts, 3 dc in next st] across to last 10 sts, dc in each of last 10 sts, turn. *(456 dc)*

Rows 19–21: Ch 3, dc in each st across, turn.

Row 22: Working in back lps, ch 3, dc in each st across, turn.

Rows 23–26: Working in both lps, ch 3, dc in each st across, turn.

Rows 27 & 28: Ch 1, sc in each st across, turn. At end of last row, fasten off.

GLOVES

Note: *Work in continuous rnds, do not join or turn unless otherwise stated. Mark first st of each rnd.*

Rnd 1: Ch 12, sl st in first ch to form ring, ch 1, sc in each ch around. *(12 sc)*

Rnds 2–20: Sc in each st around. At end of last rnd, join with sl st in beg sc. Fasten off.

FINISHING

1. Using beading needle and sewing thread, starting and ending 5 sts from each end on row 1, sew first row of beads to rem lps of row 1 of Bodice *(see illustration)*. *Sk next row on Bodice, sew next row of beads *(see illustration)* between next 2 rows, rep from * 6 times.

2. Randomly sew 37 beads on front of Skirt and rem beads on Train.

3. Sew 3 snaps evenly spaced down back opening.

4. Sew a cl of 4 small feathers over rows 1–4 on each shoulder of Bodice.

5. Sew a cl of 6 large feathers to center of row 1 on Train.

6. Sew a cl of 4 small feathers to each end of row 11 on Train.

7. Sew 9 cls of 4 feathers each evenly spaced across row 26 on Train. ❏❏

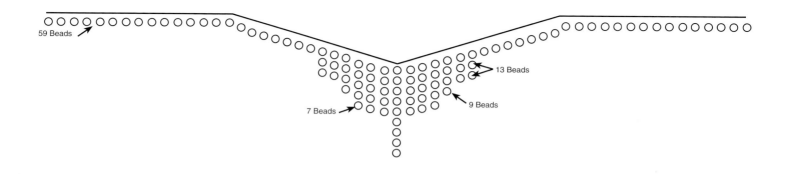

59 Beads
7 Beads
9 Beads
13 Beads

Evening Gowns

Designs by Dee Palmer

GOLD GOWN

SKILL LEVEL

INTERMEDIATE

FINISHED SIZE

Fits 11½-inch fashion doll

MATERIALS

- ❏ Metallic crochet cotton size 10: 109 yds gold
- ❏ Size 7/1.65mm steel crochet hook or size needed to obtain gauge
- ❏ Sewing needle
- ❏ Gold sewing thread
- ❏ 3 small snap fasteners
- ❏ 22-inch white feather boa

GAUGE

8 sc = 1 inch; 9 sc rows = 1 inch

INSTRUCTIONS

GOWN
Bodice

Row 1: Starting at neckline, ch 56, sc in 2nd ch from hook and in each ch across, turn. *(55 sc)*

Row 2: Ch 1, sc in each of first 9 sts, for **armhole**, ch 5, sk next 10 sts, sc in each of next 17 sts, for **armhole**, ch 5, sk next 10 sts, sc in each of last 9 sts, turn. *(35 sc, 10 chs)*

Row 3: Ch 1, sc in each st and in each ch across, turn. *(45 sc)*

Rows 4–6: Ch 1, sc in each st across, turn.

Row 7: Ch 1, sc in each of first 4 sts, **sc dec** *(see Stitch Guide)* in next 2 sts, [sc in each of next 4 sts, sc dec in next 2 sts] across to last 3 sts, sc in each of last 3 sts, turn. *(38 sc)*

Row 8: Ch 1, sc in each st across, turn.

Row 9: Ch 1, sc in each of first 4 sts, sc dec in next 2 sts, [sc in each of next 4 sts, sc dec in next 2 sts] across to last 2 sts, sc in each of last 2 sts, turn. *(32 sc)*

Rows 10–13: Ch 1, sc in each st across, turn.

Row 14: Ch 1, sc in each of first 4 sts, sc dec in next 2 sts, [sc in each

BARBIE® and associated trademarks are owned by and used with permission from Mattel, Inc. ©2005 Mattel, Inc.

of next 4 sts, sc dec in next 2 sts] across to last 2 sts, sc in each of last 2 sts, turn. *(27 sc)*

Rows 15 & 16: Ch 1, sc in each st across, turn.

Skirt

Row 17: Ch 1, sc in first st, [2 sc in next st, sc in next st] across to last st, sc in last st, turn. *(40 sc)*

Rows 18–21: Ch 1, sc in each st across, turn.

Row 22: Ch 1, sc in each of first 2 sts, [2 sc in next st, sc in each of next 2 sts] across to last 2 sts, sc in each of last 2 sts, turn. *(52 sc)*

Rnd 23: Working in rnds, ch 1, sc in each st across, join with sl st in beg sc, **turn.**

Rnd 24: Ch 1, sc in each st around, join with sl st in beg sc, **turn.**

Rnd 25: Ch 1, sc in first 2 sts, [sk next st, sc in each of next 6 sts] around to last st, sk last st, join with sl st in beg sc, turn. *(44 sc)*

Rnds 26–34: Ch 1, sc in each st around, join with sl st in beg sc, turn.

Rnd 35: Ch 1, sc in first st, sc in each of next 7 sts, [sk next st, sc in each of next 8 sts] around, join with sl st in beg sc, turn. *(40 sc)*

Rnds 36–42: Ch 1, sc in each st around, join with sl st in beg sc, turn.

Rnd 43: Ch 1, sc in first st, sc in each of next 6 sts, [sk next st, sc in each of next 7 sts] around to last st, sc in last st, join with sl st in beg sc, turn. *(36 sc)*

Rnds 44–46: Ch 1, sc in each st around, join with sl st in beg sc, turn.

Rnd 47: Ch 1, sc in first st, sc in next st, [2 sc in next st, sc in each of next 3 sts] around to last 2 sts, 2 sc in next st, sc in last st, join with sl st in beg sc, turn. *(45 sc)*

Rnds 48–76: Ch 1, sc in each st around, join with sl st in beg sc, turn. At end of last rnd, fasten off.

Finishing

1. Place Gown on doll to determine placement of snaps; sew snaps to back opening.

2. Drape feather boa across doll's shoulders, tucking under arms if desired.

BLACK GOWN
SKILL LEVEL

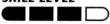

INTERMEDIATE

FINISHED SIZE
Fits 11½-inch fashion doll

MATERIALS
- ❑ Metallic crochet cotton size 10: 109 yds black
- ❑ Size 7/1.65mm steel crochet hook or size needed to obtain gauge
- ❑ Sewing needle
- ❑ Black sewing thread
- ❑ 3 small snap fasteners
- ❑ 27-inch black feather boa

GAUGE
8 sc = 1 inch; 9 sc rows = 1 inch

INSTRUCTIONS
GOWN
Bodice

Row 1: Starting at neckline, ch 56, sc in 2nd ch from hook, sc in each of next 8 chs, dc in each of next 10 chs, sc in each of next 17 chs, dc in each of next 10 chs, sc in each of last 9 chs, turn. *(35 sc, 20 dc)*

Row 2: Ch 1, sc in each of first 9 sts, for **armhole**, ch 5, sk next 10 sts, sc in each of next 17 sts, for **armhole**, ch 5, sk next 10 sts, sc in each of last 9 sts, turn. *(35 sc, 10 chs)*

Rows 3–16: Rep same rows of Gold Gown Bodice.

Skirt

Rows 17–25: Work rows 17-25 of Gold Gown Skirt.

Rnds 26–72: Ch 1, sc in each st around, join with sl st in beg sc. At end of last rnd, fasten off.

Finishing

1. Place dress on doll to determine placement of snaps; sew snaps to back opening.

2. Cut a length of feather boa long enough to go around bottom of Gown, sew to bottom of Gown.

3. Drape feather boa across doll's shoulders, tucking under arms if desired. ❑❑

Mile-a-Minute Afghan

Design by Maggie Weldon

SKILL LEVEL

INTERMEDIATE

FINISHED SIZE
8¾ x 11½ inches

MATERIALS
- ❑ Fine (sport) weight yarn:
  1 oz/90 yds/28g white
  1 oz/90 yds/28g blue
- ❑ Size F/5/3.75 crochet hook or size needed to obtain gauge
- ❑ Tapestry needle

GAUGE
11 dc = 2 inches; each Panel is 1½ inches wide x 11½ inches long

SPECIAL STITCHES
Popcorn (pc): 4 dc in st, drop lp from hook, insert hook in top of first dc of group, pull dropped lp through st.

Reverse popcorn stitch (rpc): 4 dc in st, drop lp from hook, insert hook from back to front in top of first dc of group, pull dropped lp through st.

Join with double crochet (join with dc): Place sl knot on hook, yo, insert hook in st, yo, pull lp through, (yo, pull through 2 lps on hook) twice.

INSTRUCTIONS
AFGHAN
Panel A
Make 3.
Row 1: With white, ch 5, **pc** (*see Special Stitches*) in 4th ch from hook, dc in last ch, turn. (*1 pc, 2 dc*)

Row 2: Ch 3 (*counts as first dc*), **rpc** (*see Special Stitches*) in pc, dc in 5th of ch-5, turn.

Row 3: Ch 3, pc in rpc, dc in 3rd ch of ch-3, turn.

Row 4: Ch 3, rpc in pc, dc in 3rd ch of ch-3, turn.

Rows 5–21: Rep rows 3 and 4 alternately, ending with row 3. At end of last row, **do not turn.** Fasten off.

SKIPPER® and associated trademarks are owned by and used with permission from Mattel, Inc. ©2005 Mattel, Inc.

Rnd 22: Working around outer edge, **join blue with dc** (*see Special Stitches*) in first ch of starting ch at bottom of pc on row 1, 8 dc in same ch, working across long edge, 3 dc in end of first row, [2 dc in end of next row, 3 dc in end of next row] across, 9 dc in top of pc on last row, working across long edge, 3 dc in end of next row, [2 dc in end of next row, 3 dc in end of next row] across, join with sl st in top of beg dc. Leaving a long end for sewing, fasten off.

Panel B
Make 2.
Row 1: With blue, ch 5, pc in 4th ch from hook, dc in last ch, turn. (*1 pc, 2 dc*)

Row 2: Ch 3, rpc in pc, dc in 5th ch of ch-5, turn.

Row 3: Ch 3, pc in rpc, dc in 3rd of ch-3, turn.

Row 4: Ch 3, rpc in pc, dc in 3rd ch of ch-3, turn.

Rows 5–21: Rep rows 3 and 4 alternately, ending with row 3. At end of last row, **do not turn.** Fasten off.

Rnd 22: Working around outer edge, join white with dc in ch of starting ch at bottom of pc on row 1, 8 dc in same ch, working across long edge, 3 dc in end of first row, [2 dc in end of next row, 3 dc in end of next row] across, 9 dc in top of pc on last row, working across long edge, 3 dc in end of next row, [2 dc in end of next row, 3 dc in end of next row] across, join with sl st in top of first dc. Leaving a long end for sewing, fasten off.

Assembly
Matching long edges, lay Panels side by side in this order: A, B, A, B, A.

Using tapestry needle threaded with long end of yarn, working through **back lps** (*see Stitch Guide*), sew dc sts tog across matching long edges of Panels, leaving 9 dc on each short end unsewn.

Edging
Working around entire outer edge in sts and in seams, with RS facing, join white with sc in top of seam between first 2 Panels, ch 3, [sk next st or seam, sc in next st or seam, ch 3] around, join with sl st in beg sc. Fasten off. ❑❑

Movie Star

Designs by Tammy Campbell

SKILL LEVEL

INTERMEDIATE

FINISHED SIZE

Fits 11½-inch fashion doll

MATERIALS

- ❑ Crochet cotton size 10:
   350 yds red
- ❑ Size 6/1.80mm steel crochet hook or size needed to obtain gauge
- ❑ Sewing needle
- ❑ Red sewing thread
- ❑ Seed beads:
   Red
   Clear
- ❑ Red boa feather
- ❑ Craft glue

GAUGE

8 sts = 1 inch; 4 hdc rows = 1 inch

INSTRUCTIONS

DRESS

Skirt

Row 1: Ch 24, sc in 2nd ch from hook and in each ch across, turn. *(23 sc)*

Row 2: Ch 2 *(counts as first hdc)*, hdc in same st, [hdc in next st, 2 hdc in next st] across, turn. *(35 hdc)*

Row 3: Ch 2, hdc in each st across, turn.

Row 4: Ch 2, hdc in same st, [hdc in each of next 2 sts, 2 hdc in next st] across to last st, hdc in last st, turn. *(47 hdc)*

Rows 5–8: Ch 2, hdc in each st across, turn.

Rnd 9: Working in rnds, ch 2, hdc in each st around, sk first 3 sts, join with sl st in top of 4th st. *(44 hdc)*

Rnd 10: Working through both thicknesses as needed, ch 2, hdc in each st around, join with sl st in top of beg ch-2. Fasten off.

Row 11: Working in rows, sk first 21 sts, join with sl st in next st, ch 2, hdc in each st across, turn.

Rows 12–17: Ch 2, hdc in same st, hdc in each st across, turn. *(50 hdc at end of row 17)*

BARBIE® and associated trademarks are owned by and used with permission from Mattel, Inc. ©2005 Mattel, Inc.

Row 18: Ch 2, hdc in each of first 7 sts, **hdc dec** *(see Stitch Guide)* in next 2 sts, [hdc in each of next 8 sts, hdc dec in next 2 sts] across, turn. *(45 hdc)*

Row 19: Ch 2, hdc in each of next 6 sts, hdc dec in next 2 sts, [hdc in each of next 7 sts, hdc dec in next 2 sts] across, turn. *(40 hdc)*

Row 20: Rep row 18. *(36 hdc)*

Row 21: Ch 2, hdc in each st across, turn.

Row 22: Ch 2, hdc in each of next 6 sts, hdc dec in next 2 sts, [hdc in each of next 7 sts, hdc dec in next 2 sts] across, turn. *(32 hdc)*

Row 23: Rep row 18.

Row 24: Ch 2, [hdc dec in next 2 sts, hdc in each of next 8 sts] across to last st, hdc in last st, turn. *(29 hdc)*

Rows 25–35: Ch 2, hdc in each st across, turn.

Row 36: Ch 1, sc in each st across. Fasten off.

Bodice

Row 1: Working in starting ch on opposite side of row 1 on Skirt, join with sl st in first ch, (ch 2, hdc) in same st, [2 hdc in next ch, hdc in next ch] across, turn. *(35 hdc)*

Row 2: Ch 2, hdc in each st across, turn.

First Side

Row 3: Ch 2, hdc in each of next 16 sts leaving rem sts unworked, turn. *(17 hdc)*

Row 4: Ch 2, [2 hdc in next st, hdc in next st] across, turn. *(25 hdc)*

Rows 5 & 6: Ch 2, hdc in each st across, turn.

Row 7: Ch 2, hdc in each of next 9 sts, for **armhole**, ch 6, sk next 4 sts, hdc in each of last 11 sts, turn.

Row 8: Ch 2, hdc in each st and in each ch across, turn. *(27 hdc)*

Row 9: Ch 2, hdc in each of next 2 sts, hdc dec in next 2 sts, [hdc in each of next 3 sts, hdc dec in next 2 sts] across to last 7 sts, hdc in each of last 7 sts, turn. *(23 hdc)*

Row 10: Ch 2, hdc in next st, [hdc dec in next 2 sts, hdc in next st] across, turn. Fasten off. *(16 hdc)*

Second Side

Row 3: Sk next unworked st on row 2, join with sl st in next st, ch 2, hdc in each st across, turn. *(17 hdc)*

Rows 4–10: Rep rows 4–10 of First Side.

Both Sides

Row 11: Working across both sides, join with sc in first st, [**sc dec** *(see Stitch Guide)* in next 2 sts, sc in next st] across First Side, ch 4, sc in next st on Second Side, [sc dec in next 2 sts, sc in next st] across, turn. *(22 sc, 4 chs)*

Row 12: Ch 1, sc dec in first 2 sts, [sc dec in next 2 sts or chs] across, turn. *(13 sc)*

Row 13: Ch 1, sc in each st across. Fasten off.

Sew snaps evenly spaced down back opening on Bodice.

Sleeves

Rnd 1: Join with sl st in first skipped st on armhole, ch 2, evenly sp 13 more hdc around armhole, join with sl st in top of beg ch-2. *(14 hdc)*

Rnds 2–15: Ch 1, hdc in each st around, join with sl st in top of beg hdc.

Rnd 16: Ch 1, sc in each st around, join with sl st in first sc. Fasten off.

Rep on other armhole.

HAT

Row 1: Ch 2, 4 sc in 2nd ch from hook, turn. *(4 sc)*

Rows 2 & 3: Ch 2, hdc in same st, hdc in each st across to last st, 2 hdc in last st, turn. *(8 hdc at end of row 3)*

Row 4: Ch 2, hdc in same st, 2 hdc in each st across, turn. *(16 hdc)*

Rows 5–8: Ch 2, hdc in each st across, turn.

Row 9: Ch 2, [hdc dec in next 2 sts, hdc in next st] across, turn. *(11 hdc)*

Rows 10 & 11: Ch 2, hdc in next st, [hdc dec in next 2 sts, hdc in next st] across, turn. *(6 hdc at end of row 11)*

Row 12: Ch 1, sc in each st across. Fasten off.

FINISHING

1. Glue feather along 1 long edge on Hat.

2. Sew clear beads to edge on both sides of front slit on Skirt. Sew 11 beads in a circle at top of slit.

3. Sew clear beads in a spiral around each Sleeve as shown in photo.

4. Sew clear beads around opening on front of Bodice.

5. Beg at neck edge, sew beads in rows across neck as follows: 1 row red, 2 rows clear, 2 rows red. ❏❏

Rugs

Designs by Deborah Levy-Hamburg

FINISHED SIZE
Each Rug is 7 inches across

MATERIALS
❑ Cotton fine (sport) weight
yarn:
  50 yds blue
  50 yds green
  50 yds white
  50 yds variegated
❑ Size F/5/3.75mm crochet hook
or size needed to obtain gauge

GAUGE
Rnds 1 and 2 = 1¾ inches across

SPECIAL STITCHES
Beginning cluster (beg cl): Ch
3, [yo, insert hook in same ch sp
as ch 3, yo, pull through, yo, pull
through 2 lps on hook] twice, yo,
pull through all lps on hook.

Cluster (cl): Yo, insert hook in next
ch sp, yo, pull through, yo, pull
through 2 lps on hook, [yo, insert
hook in same ch sp, yo, pull through,
yo, pull through 2 lps on hook] twice,
yo, pull through all lps on hook.

INSTRUCTIONS
RUG A
Rnd 1: With green, ch 5, sl st in first
ch to form ring, ch 3 *(counts as first
dc)*, 23 dc in ring, join with sl st in
3rd ch of beg ch-3. Fasten off.

Rnd 2: Working in back bar of dc,
join blue with sl st in first st, ch 3, dc
in same st, 2 dc in each st around,
join with sl st in 3rd ch of beg ch-3.
Fasten off.

Rnd 3: Join white with sc between 2
sts worked in same st, ch 1, sk next
2 sts, [sc between last and next st,
ch 1, sk next 2 sts] around, join with
sl st in beg sc. Fasten off.

Rnd 4: Join green with sc in any ch
sp, sc in same ch sp, ch 1, (2 sc, ch
1) in each ch sp around, join with
sl st in beg sc.

Rnd 5: (Sl st, ch 3–*counts as first hdc
and ch 1*, hdc) in next st, sk next st,
ch 1, *(hdc, ch 1, hdc) in next st,
ch 1, sk next st, rep from * around,
join with sl st in 2nd ch of beg ch-3.
Fasten off.

Rnd 6: Join white with sl st in first ch
sp, **beg cl** *(see Special Stitches)*, ch 4,
sk next ch sp, **cl** *(see Special Stitches)*,
ch 4, sk next ch sp, [cl in next ch sp,
ch 4, sk next ch sp] around, join with
sl st in top of beg cl. Fasten off.

Rnd 7: Join variegated with sl st in
any ch sp, beg cl, ch 5, [cl in next
ch sp, ch 5] around, join with sl st
in top of beg cl. Fasten off.

Rnd 8: Working over ch sps on rnd 7,
join white with sc in any cl on rnd
6, ch 5, (cl, ch 2, cl, ch 2, cl) in next
ch sp on rnd 7, ch 5, *working over
next ch sp, sc in cl on rnd 6, ch 5,
(cl, ch 2, cl, ch 2, cl) in next ch sp on
rnd 7, ch 5, rep from * around, join
with sl st in beg sc. Fasten off.

Rnd 9: Join variegated with sc in
any ch sp, ch 3, [sc in next ch sp,
ch 3] around, join with sl st in beg
sc. Fasten off.

RUG B
Rnd 1: With green, ch 5, sl st in first
ch to form ring, ch 3 *(counts as first
dc)*, 23 dc in ring, join with sl st in
3rd ch of beg ch-3.

Rnd 2: Working in back bar of dc, sl
st in back bar of first st, ch 3, 2 dc in
each st around, dc back in first st, join
with sl st in 3rd ch of beg ch-3.

Rnd 3: Sl st in next st, ch 1, [sc
between last st and next st, ch 1, sk
next 2 sts] around, join with sl st in
beg sc. Fasten off.

Rnd 4: Join white with sc in any ch
sp, sc in same ch sp, ch 1, (2 sc,
1) in each ch sp around, join with
sl st in beg sc.

Rnd 5: (Sl st, ch 3–*counts as first hdc
and ch 1*, hdc) in next st, sk next st,
ch 1, *(hdc, ch 1, hdc) in next st,
ch 1, sk next st, rep from * around,
join with sl st in 2nd ch of beg ch-3.
Fasten off.

Rnd 6: Join variegated with sl st
in first ch sp, **beg cl** *(see Special
Stitches)*, ch 4, sk next ch sp, **cl** *(see
Special Stitches)*, ch 4, sk next ch
sp, [cl in next ch sp, ch 4, sk next
ch sp] around, join with sl st in top
of beg cl.

Rnd 7: Sl st in next ch sp, beg cl, ch
5, [cl in next ch sp, ch 5] around,
join with sl st in top of beg cl.

Rnd 8: (Sl st, beg cl, ch 2, cl, ch 2,
cl) in next ch sp, ch 5, working over
next ch sp, sc in next cl on rnd 6,
ch 5, *(cl, ch 2, cl, ch 2, cl) in next
ch sp on rnd 7, ch 5, working over
next ch sp, sc in next cl on rnd 6,
ch 5, rep from * around, join with
sl st in beg sc. Fasten off.

Rnd 9: Join white with sc in any ch
sp, ch 3, [sc in next ch sp, ch 3]
around, join with sl st in beg sc.
Fasten off. ❑❑

Pearls & Lace Bride

Designs by Beverly Mewhorter

FINISHED SIZE

Fits 11½-inch fashion doll

MATERIALS

- ❏ Crochet cotton size 10: 500 yds white
- ❏ Size 7/1.65mm steel crochet hook or size needed to obtain gauge
- ❏ Tapestry needle
- ❏ Sewing needle
- ❏ Sewing thread
- ❏ 27 white teardrop beads
- ❏ Sequins
- ❏ 3mm pearl beads
- ❏ Bridal appliqués
- ❏ 2 yds 1½-inch scalloped lace
- ❏ 8 inches ¼-inch-wide lace
- ❏ 2 straight pins
- ❏ Floral spray accessories
- ❏ 2 squares of netting, each 4 inches long
- ❏ 2 yds 3mm strung pearl beads
- ❏ 1½ yds ⅛-inch-wide ribbon
- ❏ Ribbon roses:
    - 1 large
    - 24 medium
    - 30 small
- ❏ 4-inch piece white chenille stem
- ❏ Craft glue
- ❏ 28-gauge wire

GAUGE

3 V-sts = 1 inch; 4 rows = 1 inch

SPECIAL STITCHES

V-stitch (V-st): (Dc, ch 1, dc) in next st.

Shell: (Dc, ch 1, dc, ch 1, dc) in next st or ch sp.

INSTRUCTIONS

DRESS

Bodice

Row 1: Ch 26, sc in 2nd ch from hook, sc in each ch across, turn. *(25 sc)*

Row 2: Ch 1, sc in first st, *sk next st,

BARBIE® and associated trademarks are owned by and used with permission from Mattel, Inc. ©2005 Mattel, Inc.

V-st *(see Special Stitches)* in next st, sc in next st, rep from * across, turn. *(8 V-sts, 9 sc)*

Row 3: Ch 4 *(counts as first dc and ch 1)*, dc in same st, [sc in ch sp of next V-st, V-st in next sc] across, turn.

Row 4: Ch 1, sc in ch sp of first V-st, [V-st in next sc, sc in ch sp of next V-st] across, turn.

Row 5: Ch 4, dc in same st, [sc in ch sp of next V-st, V-st in next sc] across, turn.

Row 6: Ch 1, sc in ch sp of first V-st, [V-st in next sc, sc in ch sp of next V-st] across, turn.

Row 7: Ch 4, dc in same st, sc in next V-st, [V-st in next sc, sc in next V-st] twice, *shell *(see Special Stitches)* in next st, sc in next V-st, rep from * twice, V-st in next sc, [sc in next V-st, V-st in next sc] across, turn.

Row 8: Ch 1, sc in first V-st, V-st in next sc, [sc in next V-st, V-st in next sc] twice, [sc in center dc of next shell, V-st in next sc] 3 times, sc in next V-st, [V-st in next sc, sc in next V-st] across, turn.

Row 9: Ch 4, dc in same st, [sc in ch sp of next V-st, V-st in next sc] across, turn.

Row 10: Ch 1, sc in first V-st, [ch 1, sc in next sc, ch 1, sc in next V-st] twice, for **armhole**, ch 16, [sc in next sc, ch 1, sc in next V-st, ch 1] 3 times, sc in next sc, for **armhole**, ch 16, [sc in next V-st, ch 1, sc in next sc, ch 1] across to last V-st, sc in last V-st, turn.

Row 11: Sc in each of first 5 sts, [sc in next ch, dc in next ch] 8 times, sc in each st across to next ch-16, [sc in next ch, dc in next ch] 8 times, sc in each st across. Fasten off.

Sleeve
Rnd 1: Join with sc in dc in V-st at armhole, evenly sp 23 more sc around, join with sl st in beg sc. *(24 sc)*

Rnd 2: Ch 1, 2 sc in each of first 6 sts, [V-st in next st, sc in next st] 6 times, 2 sc in each of last 6 sts, join with sl st in beg sc. *(30 sc, 6 V-sts)*

Rnd 3: Ch 1, sc in each of first 12 sts, [sc in next V-st, V-st in next sc] 6 times, sc in each of last 12 sts, join with sl st in beg sc.

Rnd 4: Ch 1, sc in each of first 12 sts, [V-st in next sc, sc in next V-st] 6 times, sc in each of last 12 sts, join with sl st in beg sc.

Rnd 5: Ch 1, sc in each of first 12 sts, [sc in next V-st, V-st in next sc] 6 times, sc in each of last 12 sts, join with sl st in beg sc.

Rnd 6: Ch 1, sc in first 12 sts, (V-st in next sc, sc in next V-st) 6 times, sc in last 12 sts, join with sl st in beg sc.

Rnd 7: Ch 1, **sc dec** *(see Stitch Guide)* in first 2 sts, sk ch sps, (sc dec in next 2 sts] around, join with sl st in beg sc dec. *(21 sc)*

Rnds 8 & 9: Ch 1, sc in first st, [sc dec in next 2 sts] around, join with sl st in beg sc. *(6 sc at end of rnd 9)*

Rnds 10–15: Ch 3 *(counts as first dc)*, dc in each st around, join with sl st in top of beg ch-3. At end of last rnd, fasten off.

Rep on rem armhole.

Skirt
Row 1: Working in starting ch on opposite side of row 1, join with sc in first ch, V-st in next ch, [sc in next ch, V-st in next ch] twice, sc in each of next 13 chs, [V-st in next ch, sc in next ch] across, turn. *(6 V-sts, 19 sc)*

Row 2: Ch 4, dc in same sc, sc in next V-st, [V-st in next sc, sc in next

V-st] twice, sc in each of next 13 sts, [sc in next V-st, V-st in next sc] across, turn.

Row 3: Ch 1, sc in first V-st, V-st in next sc, [sc in next V-st, V-st in next sc] twice, sc in each of next 13 sts, [sc in next V-st, V-st in next sc] across, turn.

Row 4: Ch 4, dc in same sc, sc in next V-st, [V-st in next sc, sc in next V-st] twice, sc in each of next 13 sts, [sc in next V-st, V-st in next sc] across, turn.

Row 5: Ch 1, sc in first V-st, shell in next sc, [sc in next V-st, shell in next sc] twice, sc in each of next 13 sts, [shell in next sc, sc in next V-st] across, turn. *(6 shells, 19 sc)*

Row 6: Ch 1, 2 sc in first st, sc in each st and in each ch across with 2 sc in last st, turn. *(51 sc)*

Rnd 7: Working in rnds, ch 3, 2 dc in same st, [6 dc in next st, dc in next st] 5 times, [5 dc in next st, dc in next st] 4 times, 2 dc in each of next 3 sts, dc in each of next 6 sts, 2 dc in each of next 3 sts, [dc in next st, 5 dc in next st] 4 times, [dc in next st, 6 dc in next st] around, join with sl st in top of beg ch-3. *(146 dc)*

Rnd 8: Ch 1, sc in first st, shell in next st, [sk next st, sc in next st, shell in next st] around, join with sl st in beg sc, turn.

Rnds 9–41: Sl st across to center dc of first shell, ch 1, sc in center dc, shell

BARBIE® and associated trademarks are owned by and used with permission from Mattel, Inc. ©2005 Mattel, Inc.

in next sc, [sc in center dc of next shell, shell in next sc] around, join with sl st in beg sc, turn. At end of last rnd, fasten off.

Train
Row 42: Sk next 15 shells, join with sc in center dc of next shell, shell in next sc, [sc in center dc of next shell, shell in next sc] 18 times leaving rem shells unworked, turn. *(19 shells)*

Rows 43–45: Sl st across to center dc of first shell, ch 1, sc in center dc, shell in next sc, [sc in center dc of next shell, shell in next sc] across, turn. At end of last row, fasten off. *(5 shells)*

BUSTLE BOW
Row 1: Ch 6, sl st in first ch to form ring, ch 3, 9 dc in ring, turn.

Row 2: Ch 3, dc in same st, [dc in next st,

2 dc in next st] across. Fasten off.

Tail
Make 2.
Ch 15, sc in 2nd ch from hook, sc in next ch, hdc in each of next 2 chs, dc in each of next 4 chs, tr in each of last 6 chs. Fasten off.

FINISHING
1. For **Bustle Bow**, glue ¼-inch-wide lace to outer curved edge of Bow, glue lace around outer edges of tails. Glue sequins and 3mm pearl beads to lace as desired. Glue large ribbon rose to center of straight edge on Bow.
2. Place Dress on doll, stuff Sleeves with netting, sew back opening closed.
3. Glue sequins and 3mm beads to appliqués. Glue appliqués to Bodice and Skirt as desired.

4. Glue sequins and 3mm beads to 1½-inch-wide lace. Glue lace to bottom edge of Skirt.
5. Make 3 Teardrop Cls according to illustrations.
6. Glue 1 Teardrop Cl to each Sleeve and 1 to Bodice front as shown in photo.
7. For **necklace**, string 3mm beads onto wire, place wire around neck and twist ends tog.
8. For **earrings**, place 1 (3mm) bead and 1 sequin on each straight pin. Glue pins in ears.
9. For **veil**, twist ends of chenille stem tog to form circle. Glue ribbon roses, strung beads and ribbon around circle as shown.
10. For **bouquet**, place 12 medium and 12 small roses tog, wrap stems with ribbon. Glue lace around roses and stems.
11. Glue strung beads and floral spray to bouquet and veil. ❑❑

1. Glue 5 teardrop beads tog as shown in illustration. Glue another teardrop bead upright in center of group.

2. Cut strung beads as shown and glue 1 teardrop bead to 1 end. Glue rem end to back of cl. Make a total of 3 of these

Teardrop Cluster

Casual Comfort

Designs by Annie Potter

BARBIE® and associated trademarks are owned by and used with permission from Mattel, Inc. ©2005 Mattel, Inc.

COUCH

FINISHED SIZE
6¾ x 9¾ inches long

MATERIALS
- ❑ Medium (worsted) weight yarn: 3 oz/150 yds/85g each pale navy and white
- ❑ Size G/6/4mm crochet hook or size needed to obtain gauge
- ❑ Tapestry needle
- ❑ Foam:
    3 x 7 x 1-inch-thick piece for Bottom Cushion
    3 x 7 x ½-inch-thick piece for Top Cushion
    4 x 7 x ½-inch-thick piece for Back
    2 pieces 3¼ x 3¼ x ½-inch-thick for Arms
- ❑ Craft glue

GAUGE
4 sts = 1 inch; 3 rows of stripe pattern = 1 inch

INSTRUCTIONS

BOTTOM CUSHION
Row 1: With size G hook and white, ch 33, sc in 2nd ch from hook and in each ch across, turn. Fasten off. *(32 sc)*

Row 2: Working in **back lps** *(see Stitch Guide)* only, with pale navy, join with sl st in first st of last row, working loosely enough to keep piece flat, sl st in each st across, turn.

Row 3: Working in front lps only, ch 3 *(counts as first dc)*, dc in each st across, turn. Fasten off.

Row 4: Working in back lps only, join white with sl st in first st, sl st in each st across, turn.

Row 5: Working in **front lps** *(see Stitch Guide)* only, ch 1, sc in each st across, turn. Fasten off.

Notes: Stripe pattern is established. The front of the odd-numbered rows is the RS of the work.

Rows 6–25: Rep rows 2–5 consecutively 5 more times.

Row 26: With RS of work facing and working in rem lps of starting ch at bottom of row 1, join white with sl st in first ch, sl st in each ch across. Fasten off.

With pale navy, sew ends of rows on Cushion piece tog. Insert foam piece for Bottom Cushion. *(Foam should fit snugly inside Cushion.)*

TOP CUSHION
Row 1: With size G hook and white, ch 29, sc in 2nd ch from hook and in each ch across, turn. Fasten off. *(28 sc)*

Row 2: Working this row in back lps only, join pale navy with sl st in first st of last row, working loosely enough to keep piece flat, sl st in each st across, turn.

Row 3: Working in front lps only of sl sts on last row, ch 3, dc in each st across, turn. Fasten off.

Row 4: Working this row in back lps only, join white with sl st in first st, sl st in each st across, turn.

Row 5: Working in front lps only, ch 1, sc in each st across, turn. Fasten off.

Rows 6–25: Rep rows 2–5 consecutively 5 more times.

Row 26: With RS of work facing and working in starting ch across bottom of row 1, join white with sl st in first ch, sl st in each ch across. Fasten off.

With pale navy, sew ends of rows on Cushion piece tog. Insert foam piece for Bottom Cushion. *(Foam should fit snugly inside Cushion.)*

BACKREST
Front Piece
Row 1: With size G hook and white, ch 61, sc in 2nd ch from hook and in each ch across, turn. Fasten off. *(60 sc)*

Row 2: Working this row in back lps only, join pale navy with sl st in first st, working loosely enough to keep piece flat, sl st in each st across, turn.

Row 3: Working in front lps only, ch 3, dc in each st across, turn. Fasten off.

Row 4: Working this row in back lps only, join white with sl st in first st, sl st in each st across, turn.

Row 5: Working in front lps only, ch 1, sc in each st across, turn. Fasten off.

Rows 6–25: Rep rows 2–5 consecutively 5 more times.

First End & Flap

Row 1: Working this row in back lps only of last row, join pale navy with sl st in first st, sl st in each of next 15 sts, ch 16, turn.

Row 2: Dc in 4th ch from hook, dc in next 12 ch *(Flap completed)*, working in front lps only of sl sts on last row, dc in each st across. Fasten off.

Second End & Flap

Row 1: With RS of work facing and working in starting ch across bottom of row 1 on Front Piece, join white with sl st in first ch, sl st in each ch across, turn. Fasten off.

Row 2: Ch 14, working in front lps only, sk first 44 sts of last row, join pale navy with sl st in next st, sl st in each of next 15 sts, turn.

Row 3: Working in front lps only, ch 3, dc in each of next 15 sts *(End completed)*, dc in each of next 14 chs *(Flap completed)*. Fasten off.

End of each Flap should fit across to center of Front Piece. (*Note: They may overlap slightly.*)

Back Piece

Row 1: With size G hook and white, ch 17, sc in 2nd ch from hook and in each ch across, turn. Fasten off. *(16 sc)*

Row 2: Working this row in back lps only, join pale navy with sl st in first st, working loosely enough to keep piece flat, sl st in each st across, turn.

Row 3: Working in front lps only, ch 3, dc in each st across, turn. Fasten off.

Row 4: Working this row in back lps only, join white with sl st in first st, sl st in each st across, turn.

Row 5: Working in front lps only, ch 1, sc in each st across, turn. Fasten off.

Rows 6–25: Rep rows 2–5 consecutively 5 more times.

Row 26: With RS of work facing and working in starting ch across bottom of row 1, join white with sl st in first ch, sl st in each ch across. Fasten off.

Assembly

1. With pale navy, sew edge of row 1 on Back Piece to edge of Second End, sew edge of row 26 on Back Piece to edge of First End.

2. Sew ends of Flaps tog and sew top edge of Back Piece to edge of Flaps. Insert foam piece for Backrest inside assembled lower section of Backrest.

3. Loosely roll upper section of Backrest down to lower section, tack or glue rolled section to top of lower section.

ARM PIECE
Make 2.

Row 1: With size G hook and pale navy, ch 16, dc in 4th ch from hook *(first 3 chs count as first dc)* and in each ch across, turn. Fasten off. *(14 dc)*

Row 2: Working this row in back lps only, join white with sl st in first st of last row, working loosely enough to keep piece flat, sl st in each st across, turn.

Row 3: Working in front lps only, ch 1, sc in each st across, turn. Fasten off.

Row 4: Working this row in back lps only, join pale navy with sl st in first st, sl st in each st across, turn.

Row 5: Working in front lps only, ch 3, dc in each st across, turn. Fasten off.

Rows 6–13: Rep rows 2–5 consecutively twice.

Row 14: Working this row in back lps only, join white with sl st in first st, sl st in each st across, for **upper section,** ch 31, turn.

Row 15: Sc in 2nd ch from hook and in each ch and in each st across, turn. Fasten off. *(45 sc)*

Row 16: Working this row in back lps only, join pale navy with sl st in first st, sl st in each st across, turn.

Row 17: Working in front lps only, ch 3, dc in each st across, turn. Fasten off.

Rows 18–25: Rep rows 2–5 consecutively of Arm Piece twice.

Assembly

1. With pale navy, sew row 1 to the matching 14 sts on row 25, forming lower section of Arm. Insert foam for Arm inside lower section.

2. For Arm Top, with pale navy, ch 16, dc in 4th ch from hook and in each ch across. Fasten off.

3. Place Arm Top across top of lower section covering foam, tack or glue in place.

4. Loosely roll upper section down to lower section, tack or glue rolled section to top of lower section.

FINISHING

1. Tack or glue Top Cushion to Bottom Cushion (*with seams on bottom side*).

2. Tack or glue Backrest to back edges of assembled Cushions.

3. Tack or glue Arms to each end of assembled Cushions and Backrest according to photo.

RUG

SKILL LEVEL

EASY

FINISHED SIZE
4½ x 7 inches

MATERIALS
- ❑ Fine (baby) weight yarn:
  1¼ oz/219 yds/35g white
- ❑ Size F/5/3.75mm crochet hook or size needed to obtain gauge

GAUGE
Size F hook and 2 strands baby yarn: 9 sts = 2 inches; 5 rows =1 inch

SPECIAL STITCH
Loop stitch (lp st): Insert hook in st, wrap yarn over finger from back to front (*see illustration*) forming a lp the length needed, cross hook over front strand of lp, pick up back strand and pull through st, drop lp from finger, yo, pull through both lps on hook.

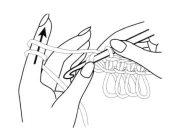

Loop Stitch

INSTRUCTIONS
RUG

Rnd 1: Holding 2 strands white tog as 1, ch 13, making ½-inch lps (**lp st**—*see Special Stitch,* sc, lp st) in 2nd ch from hook, lp st in each of next 10 chs, (lp st, sc) twice in next ch, working on opposite side of ch, lp st in each of next 10 chs, (lp st, sc) in next ch. *(30 sts)*

Rnd 2: Lp st in next st, (lp st, sc) in next st, lp st in each of next 10 sts, (lp st, sc) in each of next 2 sts, lp st in next st, (lp st, sc) in each of next 2 sts, lp st in each of next 10 sts.

Rnd 3: (Lp st, sc) in each of next 2 sts, lp st in next st, (lp st, sc) in each of next 2 sts, lp st in each of next 13 sts, (lp st, sc) in each of next 2 sts, lp st in next st, (lp st, sc) in each of next 2 sts, lp st in each of next 11 sts.

Rnd 4: *Lp st in each of next 2 sts, (lp st, sc) in next st, rep from * twice, lp st in each of next 14 sts, (lp st, sc) in next st, lp st in each of next 2 sts, (lp st, sc) in next st, lp st in each of next 2 sts, (lp st, sc) in next st, lp st in each of next 13 sts.

Rnd 5: Lp st in each of next 2 sts, *(lp st, sc) in next st, lp st in each of next 2 sts, rep from * once, (lp st, sc) in next st, lp st in each of next 17 sts, (lp st, sc) in next st, lp st in each of next 2 sts, (lp st, sc) in next st, lp st in each of next 2 sts, (lp st, sc) in next st, lp st in each of next 14 sts.

Rnd 6: Lp st in each of next 3 sts, *(lp st, sc) in next st, lp st in each of next 3 sts, rep from * twice, lp st in each of next 16 sts, (lp st, sc) in next st, lp st in each of next 3 sts, (lp st, sc) in next st, lp st in each of next 3 sts, (lp st, sc) in next st, lp st in each of next 14 sts.

Rnd 7: Lp st in each of next 5 sts, *(lp st, sc) in next st, lp in each of next 3 sts, rep from * once, (lp st, sc) in next st, lp st in each of next 21 sts, (lp st, sc) in next st, lp st in each of next 3 sts, (lp st, sc) in next st, lp st in each of next 3 sts, (lp st, sc) in next st, lp st in each of next 16 sts.

Rnd 8: Lp st in each of next 5 sts, *(lp st, sc) in next st, lp st in each of next 5 sts, rep from * once, (lp st, sc) in next st, lp st in each of next 22 sts, (lp st, sc) in next st, lp st in each of next 5 sts, (lp st, sc) in next st, lp st

in each of next 5 sts, (lp st, sc) in next st, lp st in each of next 13 sts.

Rnd 9: Lp st in each of next 7 sts, *(lp st, sc) in next st, lp st in each of next 4 sts, rep from * once, (lp st, sc) in next st, lp st in each of next 25 sts, (lp st, sc) in next st, lp st in each of next 4 sts, (lp st, sc) in next st, lp st in each of next 4 sts, (lp st, sc) in next st, lp st in each of next 18 sts.

Rnd 10: Lp st in each of next 5 sts, *(lp st, sc) in next st, lp st in each of next 4 sts*, rep between * 3 times, (lp st, sc) in next st, lp st in each of next 14 sts, rep between first * 4 times, (lp st, sc) in next st, lp st in each of last 12 sts, join with sl st in last st.

Rnd 11: Working from left to right, **reverse sc** *(see illustration)* in each st around. Fasten off.
Cut lps for shag effect.

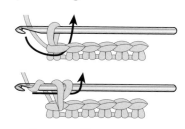

Reverse Single Crochet

PILLOWS
SKILL LEVEL
■■□▭
EASY

FINISHED SIZE
1½ inches across

MATERIALS FOR ONE EACH
- ❑ Pearl crochet cotton size 5:
  60 yds yellow
  5 yds blue
- ❑ Size 7/1.65mm steel crochet hook
- ❑ Tapestry needle
- ❑ Polyester fiberfill

SPECIAL STITCH
Slip ring (sl ring): Leaving 4-inch end on thread, lap thread over 4-inch end forming a lp, insert hook through lp from front to back, yo *(see illustration)*, pull through lp to form ring, yo, pull through lp on hook *(see illustration)*.

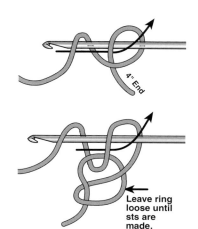

Slip Ring Stitch

INSTRUCTIONS
ROUND PILLOW
Side
Make 2.

Rnd 1: With yellow, ch 4, sl st in first ch to form ring, ch 3 *(counts as first dc)*, 11 dc in ring, join with sl st in 3rd ch of beg ch-3. *(12 dc)*

Rnd 2: Ch 3, **fpdc** *(see Stitch Guide)* around ch 3, [dc in next dc, fpdc around same dc] around, join with sl st in 3rd ch of beg ch-3. *(24 sts)*

Rnd 3: Ch 3, dc in next dc, fpdc around same dc, [fpdc around next dc, dc in next dc, fpdc around same dc] around, join with sl st in 3rd ch of beg ch-3. *(36 dc)*

Rnd 4: Ch 1, **fpsc** *(see Stitch Guide)* around ch 3, ch 2, fpdc around each dc on last rnd, join with sl st in top of beg ch-2. Fasten off.

Edging
Hold both Side pieces with WS tog, matching sts and working through **back lps** *(see Stitch Guide)* only of both layers, join blue with sl st in first st, sl st in each st around, stuffing before closing. Fasten off.

Crocheted Button
With blue, leaving long end, make a **sl ring** *(see Special Stitch)*, ch 1, work 10 sc in sl ring, pull end tightly to close ring, join with sl st in beg sc. Leaving long end, fasten off.
Weave long end through top of 10 sts, pull up tight and tie to secure.
Thread tapestry needle with 1 long end, insert needle through Pillow close to the center and pull end through.

Rep with other end, going through Pillow next to first end. Pull ends to indent center of Pillow, tie ends tog to secure. Hide ends.

SQUARE PILLOW
Side
Make 2.

Row 1: With yellow, ch 17, sc in 2nd ch from hook, dc in next ch, [sc in next, dc in next] across, turn.

Row 2: Ch 1, [sc in dc, dc in sc] across, turn.

Next rows: Rep row 2 until piece is square. At end of last row on first Side, fasten off. At end of last row on 2nd Side, **do not fasten off**.

Edging

Rnd 1: Hold both Sides tog, matching sts at ends of rows, working through both thicknesses down first edge, sc in end of each sc row and 2 sc in end of each dc row, 2 sc in corner, sc in each starting ch on opposite side of row 1, 2 sc in next corner, sc up other edge same as first edge, 2 sc in next corner, stuff Pillow, sc in each st across with 2 sc in last corner, join with sl st in beg sc.

Rnd 2: Ch 1, sc in each st around with 2 sc in 2nd st of each corner, join with sl st in beg sc. Fasten off.

Crocheted Button

With yellow, leaving long end, make a sl ring, ch 1, work 10 sc in sl ring, pull end tightly to close ring, join with sl st in beg sc. Leaving long end, fasten off.

Weave long end through top of 10 sts, pull up tight and tie to secure.

Thread tapestry needle with 1 long end, insert needle through Pillow close to the center and pull end through.

Rep with other end, going through Pillow next to first end. Pull ends to indent center of Pillow, tie ends tog to secure. Hide ends. ❏❏

Skating Fun

Designs by Mary Layfield

SKILL LEVEL

INTERMEDIATE

FINISHED SIZE
Fits 9½-inch fashion doll

MATERIALS
- ❑ Fine (sport) weight yarn:
  ½ oz/85 yds/14g turquoise
  small amount fuzzy white
- ❑ Size C/2/2.75mm crochet hook
  or size needed to obtain gauge
- ❑ Tapestry needle
- ❑ Sewing needle
- ❑ Turquoise sewing thread
- ❑ 3 inches ⅛-inch-wide
  white elastic
- ❑ 2 small snaps

GAUGE
7 sts = 1 inch; 4 dc rows = 1 inch

INSTRUCTIONS
DRESS
Bodice Front
Row 1: With turquoise, ch 14, sc in 2nd ch from hook and in each ch across, turn. *(13 sc)*

Row 2: Ch 3 *(counts as first dc)*, dc in same st, dc in each st across to last st, 2 dc in last st, turn. *(15 dc)*

Row 3: Ch 1, sc in each st across, turn.

Rows 4 & 5: Rep rows 2 and 3. *(17 dc)*

Row 6: Sl st in each of first 3 sts, ch 3, dc in each st across leaving last 3 sts unworked, turn. *(13 dc)*

Row 7: Ch 1, sc in each st across, turn.

Row 8: Ch 3, dc in each st across, turn.

First Shoulder
Row 9: Ch 1, sc in each of first 5 sts leaving rem sts unworked, turn. *(5 sc)*

Row 10: Sl st in each of first 2 sts, ch 3, dc in each st across, turn. *(4 dc)*

Row 11: Ch 1, sc in each st across, turn.

Row 12: Ch 3, dc in next st, hdc in next st, sc in last st. Fasten off.

Second Shoulder
Row 9: Sk next 3 unworked sts on row

SKIPPER® and associated trademarks are owned by and used with permission from Mattel, Inc. ©2005 Mattel, Inc.

8, join turquoise with sc in next st, sc in each st across, turn. *(5 sc)*

Row 10: Ch 3, dc in each of next 3 sts leaving last st unworked, turn. *(4 dc)*

Row 11: Ch 1, sc in each st across, turn.

Row 12: Ch 1, sc in first st, hdc in next st, dc in each of last 2 sts. Fasten off.

Bodice Back
Make 2.
Row 1: With turquoise, ch 11, sc in 2nd ch from hook, sc in each ch across, turn. *(10 sc)*

Row 2: Ch 3, dc in each st across, turn. *(10 dc)*

Row 3: Ch 1, sc in each st across, turn.

Rows 4 & 5: Rep rows 2 and 3.

Row 6: Ch 3, dc in each st across leaving last st unworked for armhole shaping, turn. *(10 dc)*

Rows 7–9: Rep rows 3 and 2 alternately, ending with row 3.

Row 10: Sl st in each of first 2 sts, ch 3, dc in each st across, turn. *(9 dc)*

Row 11: For **shoulder**, sl st in each of

first 5 sts, ch 3, dc in next st, hdc in next st, sc in last st. Fasten off.

Matching armhole shaping, sew ends of rows 1–5 of each Back to ends of rows 1–5 of Front.

Sew shoulders on Front and Backs tog, forming seams.

Collar
Working in sts and in ends of rows across neckline of Bodice, join white with sl st in first st on left Back, ch 3, evenly sp 29 dc across to right Back. Fasten off.

Sleeve
Make 2.
Row 1: With turquoise, ch 14, sc in 2nd ch from hook and in each ch across, turn. *(13 sc)*

Row 2: Ch 3, dc in each st across, turn.

Row 3: Ch 1, sc in each st across, turn.

Rows 4–7: Rep rows 2 and 3 alternately.

Row 8: Ch 3, dc in same st, dc in each of next 5 sts, 3 dc in next st, dc in each of next 5 sts, 2 dc in last st, turn. *(17 dc)*

Row 9: Sl st in each of first 2 sts, sc in next st, dc in each of next 11 sts, sc in next st leaving last 2 sts unworked, turn. *(15 sts)*

Row 10: Sl st in each of first 2 sts, sc in next st, dc in each of next 5 sts, sc in next st leaving last 4 sts unworked. Fasten off.

Fold Sleeve in half lengthwise, sew ends of rows 1–8 tog, forming underarm seam.

Cuff

Working in rem lps on opposite side of starting ch at bottom of Sleeve, join white with sl st in first ch, ch 3, dc in each ch around, join with sl st in 3rd ch of beg ch-3. Fasten off.

Easing edges to fit, sew top of Sleeve to armhole on Bodice.

Skirt

Row 1: Working in rem lps on opposite side of starting ch across bottom of Bodice, join turquoise with sl st in first ch, ch 3, 2 dc in each ch across to last ch, dc in last ch, turn. *(64 dc)*

Row 2: Ch 3, dc in each st across, turn.

Rnd 3: Working in rnds, ch 3, dc in next st, [dc in next st, 2 dc in next st] around to last 2 sts, dc in each of last 2 sts, join with sl st in 3rd ch of beg ch-3, **turn.** *(94 dc)*

Rnds 4 & 5: Ch 3, dc in each st around, join with sl st in 3rd ch of beg ch-3, turn.

Rnd 6: Rep rnd 3. Fasten off.

Rnd 7: Join white with sl st in first st, ch 3, dc in each st around, join with sl st in 3rd ch of beg ch-3. Fasten off.

SHORTS
Side
Make 2.

Rnd 1: With turquoise, ch 22, sl st in first ch to form ring, ch 1, sc in each ch around, join with sl st in beg sc, **turn.** *(22 sc)*

Rnd 2: Ch 1, sc in each of first 2 sts, ch 2 *(counts as dc)*, dc in each st across to last st, ch 1, sc in last st, join with sl st in beg sc, turn.

Row 3: Working in rows, sl st in each of first 3 sts, ch 3, dc in each st across leaving last 2 sts unworked, turn.

Rows 4 & 5: Ch 3, dc in each dc across, turn.

Row 6: Ch 1, sc in each st across. Fasten off.

Matching ends of rows and unworked sts on Sides, sew edges tog, forming front and back seam.

Stretching to fit, sew elastic to inside of top edge on Shorts.

HAT

With white, ch 21, sc in 2nd ch from hook, sc in next ch, dc in each of next 16 chs, sc in last 2 chs, ch 1, working in starting ch, sc in each of next 2 chs, dc in each of next 14 chs, sc in each of last 2 chs, ch 1, join with sl st in first sc. Fasten off.

Ties

Join white with sl st in ch-1 at 1 end of Hat, ch 24. Fasten off.

Rep on opposite end. ❏❏

Daisy Tablecloth

Design by Donna Jones

SKILL LEVEL

INTERMEDIATE

FINISHED SIZE
16 inches across

MATERIALS
- ❑ Crochet cotton size 10: 300 yds white
- ❑ Size 6/1.80mm steel crochet hook or size needed to obtain gauge

GAUGE
8 sts = 1 inch; 9 dc rows = 2 inches; Daisy is 1 inch across

SPECIAL STITCHES
Cluster (cl): *Yo, insert hook in st, yo, pull lp through, yo, pull through 2 lps on hook leaving last lps on hook, working in same st, rep from * number of times needed for number of dc in cl, yo and pull through all lps on hook.

Half cluster (half cl): Ch 4, dc in 4th ch from hook.

INSTRUCTIONS
TABLECLOTH

Rnd 1: Ch 4, 11 dc in 4th ch from hook, join with sl st in 4th ch of beg ch-4. *(12 dc)*

Rnd 2: Ch 3 *(counts as first dc)*, dc in first st, 2 dc in each st around, join with sl st in 3rd ch of beg ch-3. *(24 dc)*

Rnds 3 & 4: Ch 3, 2 dc in next st, [dc in next st, 2 dc in next st] around, join with sl st in 3rd ch of beg ch-3. *(54 dc at end of rnd 4)*

Rnd 5: Ch 3, dc in next st, 2 dc in next st, [dc in each of next 2 sts, 2 dc in next st] around, join with sl st in 3rd ch of beg ch-3. *(72 dc)*

Rnd 6: Ch 3, dc in each of next 2 sts, 2 dc in next st, [dc in each of next 3 sts, 2 dc in next st] around, join with sl st in beg ch-3. *(90 dc)*

Rnd 7: Ch 3, dc in each st around, join with sl st in 3rd ch of beg ch-3.

Rnd 8: Ch 3, dc in next st, [2 dc in next st, dc in each of next 3 sts] around, join with sl st in 3rd ch of beg ch-3. *(112 dc)*

Rnd 9: Ch 3, dc in same st, dc in each of next 6 sts, [2 dc in next st, dc in each of next 6 sts] around, join with sl st in 3rd ch of beg ch-3. *(128 dc)*

Rnd 10: Ch 6, dc in 3rd ch from hook *(counts as first half cl)*, sk next st, **3-dc cl** *(see Special Stitches)* in next st, sk next 2 sts, 3-dc cl in next st, **half cl** *(see Special Stitches)*, sk next 2 sts, *dc in next st, half cl, sk next st, 3-dc cl in next st, sk next 2 sts, 3-dc cl in next st, half cl, sk next 2 sts, rep from * around, join with sl st in 3rd ch of beg ch-6.

Rnd 11: Ch 4, sl st in top of first half cl, *[ch 4, dc in 4th ch from hook, ch 3, sl st in same ch as dc] 3 times *(3 petals made)*, sk next cl, sl st in top of next cl, ch 3, sk next half cl, sl st in next dc, ch 3, sk next half cl, sl st in top of next cl, rep from * around to last 2 cls, [ch 4, dc in 4th ch from hook, ch 3, sl st in same ch as dc] 3 times *(3 petals made)*, sk next cl, sl st in top of next cl, sk last half cl, tr in same ch as joining sl st of last rnd, **turn,** sl st across side of last petal to tip, **turn.**

Rnd 12: Ch 1, covering sl st, sc in tip of petal, *[sc in tip of next petal, ch 5] twice, sc in tip of next petal, rep from * around to last 2 petals, sc in next petal, ch 5, sc in next petal, ch 2, join with dc in first sc *(joining ch sp made)*.

Rnd 13: Ch 1, sc in joining ch sp, ch 5, [sc in next ch sp, ch 5] around, join with sl st in beg sc. *(32 sc, 32 ch sps)*

Rnd 14: Ch 3, dc in each ch and in each st around, join with sl st in 3rd ch of beg ch-3. *(192 dc)*

Rnds 15–19: Rep rnds 10–14.

Rnds 20–22: Rep rnds 10–12.

Rnd 23: Ch 1, sc in joining ch sp, ch 4, [sc in next ch sp, ch 4] around, join with sl st in beg sc. *(72 sc, 72 ch sps)*

Rnd 24: Ch 3, dc in each ch and in each st around, join with sl st in 3rd ch of beg ch-3. *(360 dc)*

Rnds 25–27: Rep rnds 10–12.

Rnds 28–30: Ch 1, sc in joining ch sp, [ch 5, sc in next ch sp] around, ch 2, join with dc in beg sc.

Rnd 31: Ch 1, sc in joining ch sp, ch 5, sc in next ch sp, ch 3, sl st in top of last sc made, ch 5, [sc in next ch sp, ch 5, sc in next ch sp, ch 3, sl st in top of last sc made, ch 5] around, join with sl st in beg sc. Fasten off. ❏❏

Old-Fashioned Star Quilt

Design by Annie Potter

SKILL LEVEL

INTERMEDIATE

FINISHED SIZE
10 x 13 inches

MATERIALS
- ❏ Crochet cotton size 10:
  - 200 yds white
  - 90 yds light green
  - 50 yds medium pink
  - 30 yds each of 12 desired colors for colors A and B
- ❏ Size 7/1.65mm steel crochet hook or size needed to obtain gauge

GAUGE
8 sts = 1 inch; 4 dc rows = 1 inch

SPECIAL STITCHES
Long single crochet (long sc): Insert hook from front to back through top of st on specified row below, working over row or rows, yo and pull up a long lp *(see illustration)*, yo and pull through both lps on hook.

Long Single Crochet

Decrease (dec): Leaving the last lp of each st on hook, dc in sk ch-1 sp, tr in the seam and dc in next sk ch-1 sp, yo and pull through all lps on hook.

INSTRUCTIONS
QUILT BLOCK
Make 12.
Block Center
Note: *This piece will be a loose circle until lps are looped.*

Rnd 1: With desired color A, ch 56, being careful not to twist ch, sl st in first ch to form ring, [sc in each of next 6 chs, ch 8, sk next ch] 8 times, join with sl st in beg sc. Fasten off.

Rnd 2: Join white with sc in 2nd sc of any 6-sc group, ch 2, dc in each of next 3 sc, ch 8, [sk over to 2nd sc of next sc group, dc in each of next 4 sc, ch 8] 7 times, join with sl st in 2nd ch of beg ch-2. Fasten off.

Rnd 3: Join desired color B with sc in 2nd dc of any 4-dc group on last rnd, ch 2, dc in next dc, ch 8, [sk over to 2nd dc of next dc group, dc in next dc, ch 8] 7 times, join with sl st in 2nd ch of beg ch- 2. Fasten off.

Looping
Starting at outer edge *(rnd 1)* and working toward center, twist first ch-8 lp on rnd 1 and pull corresponding ch-8 lp on rnd 2 through end of twisted lp, pull corresponding ch-8 lp on rnd 3 through ch-8 lp on rnd 2 *(end of this lp will be left loose until later)*.

Rep looping process with each section of ch-8 lps around circle.

Run separate strand of color B through each loose lp on rnd 3, pull up strand gathering ends of lps tog at center of circle, pulling strand tightly enough to close the opening. Tie ends of

strand tog on WS of piece to secure gathering. Hide ends.

Outer Edge
Rnd 1: Working in starting ch-56 on Block Center, join white with sc in first ch after any sk ch-1, sc in each of next 5 lps, [**long sc** *(see Special Stitches—make sure lps of st are loose enough to keep from pulling edge in)* over the next ch 1 and into the middle of the twisted ch-8 lp below, sc in next 6 lps] 7 times, long sc over last ch 1 and into the middle of the twisted ch-8 lp below, join with sl st in beg sc.

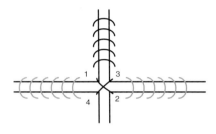

Rnd 2: Ch 1, sc in each of first 5 sts, [hdc in each of next 2 sts, 2 dc in next, 2 tr in next st, ch 1 (corner made), 2 tr in next st, 2 dc in next st, hdc in each of next 2 sts, sc in each of next 6 sts] 3 times, hdc in each of next 2 sts, 2 dc in next st, 2 tr in next st, ch 1, 2 tr in next st, 2 dc in next st, hdc in each of next 2, sc in next st, join with sl st in beg sc. Fasten off.

QUILT BLOCK ASSEMBLY
For **first strip**, matching sts, with white thread, whipstitch 1 edge of 2 Blocks tog, stitching from corner ch 1 to corner ch 1 *(do not st into ch-1 at corners yet)*. Rep adding 3 more

Blocks to strip.
Make 2 more strips the same as first strip.
Starting at corner, whipstitch edges of 2 strips tog in same manner as the Blocks, stitching into the skipped corner ch-1 sps as shown in illustration.
Rep adding the 3rd strip.

BORDER
Note: *Work all rnds in **back lps** (see Stitch Guide).*

Rnd 1: Working in outer edge of assembled Blocks, with white, join with sl st in any corner ch-1 sp, ch 4, dc in same ch-1 sp, *dc in each st across to next seam, **dec** *(see Special Stitches)*, dc in each st across to next seam, dec, dc in each st across to next corner ch-1 sp, (dc, ch 1, dc) in ch-1 sp, dc in each st across to next seam, [dec, dc in each st across to next seam] 3 times*, (dc, ch 1, dc) in corner ch-1 sp, rep between *, join with sl st in 3rd ch of beg ch-4. Fasten off.

Rnd 2: Join medium pink with sl st in any corner ch-1 sp, ch 4, dc in same ch-1 sp, dc in each st around with (dc, ch 1, dc) in each corner ch-1 sp, join with sl st in 4th ch of beg ch-4. Fasten off.

Rnd 3: Join white with sl st in any corner ch-1 sp, ch 4, (tr, ch 1, 2 tr) in same ch-1 sp, tr in each st around with (2 tr, ch 1, 2 tr) in each corner ch-1 sp, join with sl st in 4th ch of ch-4. Fasten off.

Rnd 4: With light green, rep rnd 3.

Rnd 5: With medium pink, join with sl st in any st, sl st in each st around with (sl st, ch 1, sl st) in each corner ch-1 sp. Fasten off. ❏❏

Wintertime Hats & Accessories

Designs by Deborah Levy-Hamburg

SKILL LEVEL

INTERMEDIATE

FINISHED SIZE
Fits 11½-inch fashion doll

MATERIALS
- ❏ Fine (baby) weight yarn: Small amount each of desired colors A and B, and off-white
- ❏ Size B/1/2.25mm steel crochet hook or size needed to obtain gauge
- ❏ Tapestry needle

GAUGE
Rnd 1 of Solid-Color Hat = ¾ inch across
Rnd 1 of Hat With Off-White Trim = ¾ inch across

INSTRUCTIONS
SOLID-COLOR HAT
Rnd 1: With A, ch 3, 11 dc in 3rd ch from hook *(first chs count as first dc)*, join with sl st in 3rd ch of beg ch-3. *(12 dc)*

Rnd 2: Working rnds 2 and 3 in **back lps** *(see Stitch Guide)*, ch 3 *(counts as first dc)*, dc in same st, 2 dc in each st around, join with sl st in 3rd ch of beg ch-3. *(24 dc)*

Rnd 3: Ch 3, dc in each st around, join with sl st in 3rd ch of beg ch-3.

Rnd 4: Working in both lps, ch 3, dc in each st around, join with sl st in 3rd ch of beg ch-3, turn.

Rnd 5: Ch 4 *(counts as first dc and ch 1)*, dc in same st, ch 1, sk next st, *(dc, ch 1, dc) in next st, ch 1, sk next st, rep from * around, join with sl st in 3rd ch of beg ch-4. *(24 ch sps)*

Rnd 6: Sl st in next ch and in next st, (sl st, ch 5, dc) in next ch sp, sk next ch sp, (dc, ch 1, dc) in next ch sp, sk next ch sp, *(dc, ch 2, dc) in next ch sp, sk next ch sp, (dc, ch 1, dc) in next ch sp, sk next ch sp, rep from * around, join with sl st in 3rd ch of beg ch-5. *(12 ch sps)*

Rnd 7: (Sl st, ch 3, 6 dc) in first ch-2 sp, sc in next ch-1 sp, [7 dc in next ch-2 sp, sc in next ch-1 sp] around, join with sl st in 3rd ch of beg ch-3. Fasten off.
Fold rnds 5–7 to outside for cuff.

SOLID-COLOR SCARF
Row 1: With A, ch 5, sl st in first ch to form ring, [ch 3 *(counts as first dc)*, dc, ch 1, 2 dc] in ring, turn. *(4 dc, 1 ch sp)*

Rows 2–36: Ch 3, (dc, ch 1, dc) in next ch sp, dc in 3rd ch of beg ch-3, turn.

Rnd 37: (Sc, ch 3, sc, ch 3, sc, ch 3, sc) in ch-1 sp, working in ends of rows, (sc, ch 3, sc) in each of next 2 rows, *sk next row, (sc, ch 3, sc) in next row*, rep between * across to ring on row 1, (sc, ch 3, sc, ch 3, sc, ch 3, sc) in ring, (sc, ch 3, sc) in next row, rep between * 17 times, (sc, ch 3, sc) in last row, join with sl st in beg sc. Fasten off.

KIRA® and associated trademarks are owned by and used with permission from Mattel, Inc. ©2005 Mattel, Inc.

HAT WITH OFF-WHITE TRIM

Rnd 1: With B, ch 3, 11 dc in 3rd ch from hook *(first chs count as first dc)*, join with sl st in 3rd ch of beg ch-3. *(12 dc)*

Rnd 2: (Sl st, ch 3, dc) in sp between first 2 sts, 2 dc in each sp between sts around, join with sl st in 3rd ch of beg ch-3. *(24 dc)*

Rnds 3 & 4: Sl st in sp between first 2 sts, ch 3, dc in each sp between sts around, join with sl st in 3rd ch of beg ch-3.

Rnd 5: Ch 3, dc in each st around, join with sl st in 3rd ch of beg ch-3, **turn.**

Rnds 6 & 7: Ch 1, hdc in first st, hdc in each st around, join with sl st in beg hdc. At end of last rnd, turn. Fasten off.

Rnd 8: Join off-white with sc in sp between first 2 sts, tr in same sp, (sc, tr) in each sp between sts around, join with sl st in beg sc, turn. Fasten off.

Rnd 9: Join B with sc in first st, ch 1, sk next st, [sc in next st, ch 1, sk next st) around, join with sl st in beg sc. Fasten off. Fold rnds 7–9 to outside for cuff.

SCARF WITH OFF-WHITE TRIM

Row 1: With B, ch 4, dc in 3rd ch from hook *(first 3 chs count as first dc)*, ch 1, 2 dc in last ch, turn. *(4 dc, 1 ch sp)*

Rows 2–36: Ch 3 *(counts as first dc)*, (dc, ch 1, dc) in next ch sp, dc in 3rd ch of beg ch-3, turn. At end of row 36, **do not turn.**

Rnd 37: Working in ends of rows, ch 1, (hdc, ch 1, hdc) in end of each row across, (hdc, ch 1, hdc) 3 times in sp between 2nd and 3rd dc of row 1, (hdc, ch 1, hdc) in end of each row across, (hdc, ch 1, hdc) 3 times in ch-1 sp of row 36, join with sl st in first hdc, **turn.** Fasten off.

Row 38: Join off-white with sc in first ch-1 sp, (tr, sc) in same sp, (sc, tr, sc) in each ch sp around, join with sl st in beg sc. Fasten off.

MITTEN
Make 2.

Row 1: With desired color to match Hat and Scarf, ch 16, sl st in 2nd ch from hook, sl st in each of next 2 chs, sc in each of next 4 chs, sl st in next ch, sc in each of next 4 chs, sl st in each of last 3 chs, turn. *(15 sc and sl sts)*

Rows 2 & 3: Working rem rows in back lps, ch 1, sl st in each of first 3 sts, sc in each of next 4 sts, sl st in next st, sc in each of next 4 sts, sl st in each of last 3 sts, turn.

Row 4: Ch 1, sl st in each of first 3 sts, sc in each of next 2 sts, for **thumb**, ch 1, sk next 5 sts, sc in each of next 2 sts, sl st in each of last 3 sts, turn. *(11 sts and chs)*

Row 5: Ch 1, sl st in each of first 3 sts, sc in each of next 2 sts, sl st in next st, sc in each of next 2 sts, sl st in each of last 3 sts. Leaving a 10-inch strand for sewing, fasten off.

Fold Mitten in half matching ends of rows. With needle and 10-inch strand, sew back lps of row 5 tog, run needle through thumb and sew back lps of unworked sts on row 4 tog, run needle through sl sts at fold, sew opposite side of starting ch tog. ❏❏

Annie's Attic

306 East Parr Road
Berne, IN 46711
© 2005 Annie's Attic

TOLL-FREE ORDER LINE or to request a free catalog (800) LV-ANNIE (800) 582-6643
Customer Service (800) AT-ANNIE (800) 282-6643, **Fax** (800) 882-6643
Visit www.AnniesAttic.com

ISBN: 1-59635-054-7
Printed in USA   1 2 3 4 5 6 7 8 9

Stitch Guide

ABBREVIATIONS

beg ....begin/beginning
bpdc ....back post double crochet
bpsc .... back post single crochet
bptr.............back post treble crochet
CC ....contrasting color
ch ....chain stitch
ch- .... refers to chain or space previously made (i.e. ch-1 space)
ch sp .... chain space
cl(s) ....cluster(s)
cm ....centimeter(s)
dc ....double crochet
dec..decrease/decreases/decreasing
dtr....................double treble crochet
fpdc ....front post double crochet
fpsc .... front post single crochet
fptr...............front post treble crochet
g .... gram(s)
hdc ....half double crochet
inc ......increase/increases/increasing
lp(s)....................................loop(s)
MC ....main color
mm .... millimeter(s)
oz.................................ounce(s)
pc .... popcorn
rem .... remain/remaining
rep .... repeat(s)
rnd(s) .... round(s)
RS...................................right side
sc .... single crochet
sk .... skip
sl st ....slip stitch
sp(s) ....space(s)
st(s) ....stitch(es)
tog.................................together
tr ....treble crochet
trtr..............................triple treble
WS.................................. wrong side
yd(s)..yard(s)
yo .... yarn over

Chain—ch: Yo, pull through lp on hook.

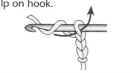

Slip s i ch—sl s : Insert hook in st, o, pull through both lps on hook.

Single croche —sc: Insert hook in st, o, pull through st, o, pull through both lps on hook.

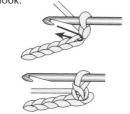

Front loop—front lp
Back loop—back lp

Front Loop   Back Loop

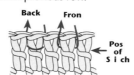

Fron pos s i ch—fp:
Back pos s i ch—bp: When working post st, insert hook from right to left around post st on previous row.

Back   Fron

Pos of S i ch

Half double crochet—hdc: Yo, insert hook in st, o, pull through st, o, pull through all 3 lps on hook.

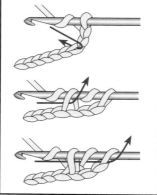

Double croche —dc: Yo, insert hook in st, o, pull through st, [o, pull through 2 lps] twice.

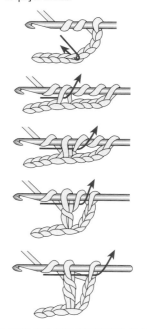

t hange colors: Drop first color; with 2nd color, pull through last 2 lps of st.

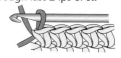

Treble crochet—tr: Yo twice, insert hook in st, yo, pull through st, [yo, pull through 2 lps] 3 times.

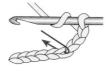

Double treble crochet—dtr: Yo 3 times, insert hook in st, o, pull through st, [o, pull through 2 lps] 4 times.

Single crochet decrease (sc dec): (Insert hook, o, draw up a lp) in each of the sts indicated, o, draw through all lps on hook.

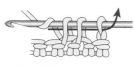

Example of 2-sc dec

Half double crochet decrease (hdc dec): (Yo, insert hook, o, draw lp through) in each of the sts indicated, o, draw through all lps on hook.

Example of 2-hdc dec

Double crochet decrease (dc dec): (Yo, insert hook, o, draw lp through, o, draw through 2 lps on hook) in each of the sts indicated, o, draw through all lps on hook.

Example of 2-dc dec

US		UK
(p stitch)	=	sc (single crochet)
sc (single crochet)	=	dc (double crochet)
hdc (half double crochet)	=	htr (half treble crochet)
dc (double crochet)	=	tr (treble crochet)
tr (treble crochet)	=	dtr (double treble crochet)
dtr (double treble crochet)	=	ttr (triple treble crochet)
skip	=	miss

For more complete information, visit

StitchGuide.com